VIRTUAL REALITY
COMPUTERS MIMIC
THE PHYSICAL WORLD

SEAN M. GRADY

Facts On File, Inc.

Virtual Reality: Computers Mimic the Physical World

Copyright © 1998 by Sean M. Grady

Facts On File, Inc.
11 Penn Plaza
New York, NY 10001

Library of Congress Cataloging-in-Publication Data

Grady, Sean M., 1965–
    Virtual reality : computers mimic the physical world / Sean M. Grady.
        p.   cm. — (Facts on File science sourcebooks)
    Includes bibliographical references and index.
    ISBN 0-8160-3605-5
    1. Human-computer interaction—Juvenile literature.   2. Virtual reality—
Juvenile literature.   I. Title.   II. Series.
    QA76.9.H85G719 1998
    006—dc21   97-15813

Facts On File books are available at special discounts when purchased in bulk quantities for businesses, associations, institutions, or sales promotions. Please call our Special Sales Department in New York at (212) 967-8800 or (800) 322-8755.

You can find Facts On File on the World Wide Web at http://www.factsonfile.com

Text design by Cathy Rincon
Cover design by Amy Gonzalez
Illustrations on pages 7, 10, and 22 by Jeremy Eagle
On the cover: The CAVE environment used to design the Caterpillar 914G wheel loader (courtesy Kem Ahlers, Manager of University Relations, Caterpillar Inc.).

Printed in the United States of America

MP FOF 10 9 8 7 6 5 4 3 2 1

This book is printed on acid-free paper.

CONTENTS

Acknowledgments   vi

1 Immersion in Alternate Worlds   1
    What Is Virtual Reality?   3
    How Does Virtual Reality Work?   6
    A Quick Tour of VR   8
    Immersing the Audience   9
    Entertaining the Senses   13

2 The Path to Virtual Reality   15
    A New Way to Control Computers   15
    Easier Interactions with Early Computers   17
    "The Ultimate Display"   19
    Simulating Flight   20
    "Darth Vader" in the Cockpit   24

3 Simulating Reality   26
    Putting People in Artificial Realities   27
    Remaking Reality at NASA   29
    A New View of Computer Data   31
    Naming the Future of Computing   35

4 The Tools of VR   37
    Reality in a Box   37
    Trackers: Where in the (Virtual) World Are You?   39
    Virtual Visualization   41
    Three-Dimensional Sound   45

Touching Objects in Thin Air: Manipulation Devices 46
Working in Wide-Open Spaces: Projection-Based VR 50
Augmented Reality 52

5 Virtual Architecture 53
Altering Virtual Office Buildings 54
Detecting Design Flaws with Virtual Reality 57
Escaping Disaster with VR Design 59
A Virtually Guaranteed Presentation 60
Buildings for a Virtual World 61

6 Science and Engineering with VR 64
Getting a Feel for Microscopic Worlds 65
Exploring Other Planets via VR 69
VR and Scientific Visualization 71
Running Experiments in Virtual Labs 73
Blowing in the (Virtual) Wind 74
Engineering: Blowing in the (Virtual) Wind, Part II 75
Creating Better Construction Equipment with VR 77
Comfort and Convenience, Courtesy of VR 80

7 Medicine and VR 82
Medical Training with VR 82
Preparing for Real Surgery 85
Safer Surgery through Simulation 87
VR in the OR 88
Physical Therapy in a Virtual World 91
Fighting Phobias in a Safe Environment 93

8 VR in the Business World 96
Virtually Sound Investments 96
Changing Store Layouts via VR 101
Meeting Clients Virtually Anywhere 103
Shopping for a House with VR 106
Virtual Offices in Virtual Reality? 106

9 Learning, Training, and Playing in VR 108
VR in the Classroom 109

Touring the Past with VR   112
VR on Campus   113
High-Tech Training in Virtual Environments   115
Virtual Industrial Training   118
VR and Entertainment   119
Virtual Worlds within a Virtual World   121
VR Gaming at Home   123

10 Virtual Reality in the Military   125
Beyond SuperCockpit   126
A Wide DIStribution of Military VR   128
Individual Tactics in a Virtual Combat Zone   129
To the Sea in Simulated Ships   133
DOOMed to Oppose the Marines   134

11 Real Drawbacks to Virtual Reality   136
Cyberhype: Mistaking Pipe Dreams for Predictions   137
The Physical Drawbacks of Virtual Reality   139
Cyberspace Sickness   140
Decompressing from VR   141
Blurring the Definition of Reality   143

12 A Virtually Certain Future for VR   145
A Prediction of Virtual Prosperity   146
A Virtual Presence in Simulated Spaces   148
Combining the Best of Both Worlds   152
A Final Note   155

Glossary   156

Further Reading   165

Index   167

ACKNOWLEDGMENTS

I wish to thank all those who provided their assistance as I researched and wrote this book. In particular, I wish to thank: Dace Campbell and Alden Jones of the Human Interface Technology Lab; Dr. Gary Bishop and Linda Houseman of the University of North Carolina at Chapel Hill; Dr. Tom DeFanti and Dr. Maxine Brown of the University of Chicago's Electronic Visualization Laboratory; Dr. Donald H. Sanders of Learning Sites Inc.; Kem Ahlers of Caterpillar Inc.; Bill Aulet of SensAble Technologies Inc.; John Bluck of NASA's Ames Research Center; James Hartsfield and Becky Fryday of NASA's Johnson Space Center; Dr. Veronica Pantelidis of East Carolina University's Virtual Reality and Education Laboratory; Dr. Terry Marsh of Quantal International Inc.; Paul Marshall of Maxus Systems International; Larry D. Sieck of the San Diego Data Processing Corporation; Valerie Minard of the MIT Media Lab.; 1st Lt. Scott Gordon, former spokesman, United States Marine Corps Systems Command; Dr. John Bell and Professor H. Scott Fogler, Department of Chemical Engineering, University of Michigan; and Becky Underwood, Kelly Walsh High School, Casper, Wyoming.

1

IMMERSION IN
ALTERNATE WORLDS

*I*n 1965, Ivan Sutherland, a pioneer in the then-new field of computer graphics, created a device that allowed people to interact with computers in a novel way. The device, which hung from the ceiling on a pivoting metal post, sat like a helmet on a person's head. Using a set of glass prisms, it reflected computer-generated images of objects from two small video monitors hanging beside the user's head into the user's eyes. The user's brain blended the two separate images into one, giving the impression that a three-dimensional object was floating in mid-air. Even more remarkably, the device—called a *head-mounted display*, or HMD—displayed different views of the object as the user's head moved. Sensors attached to the HMD constantly monitored which way the user was looking, and allowed the user to examine the object from many angles.

Sutherland's device was a radical departure from normal computer interfaces. For most of the previous two decades, using computers had been tedious and time-consuming. Com-

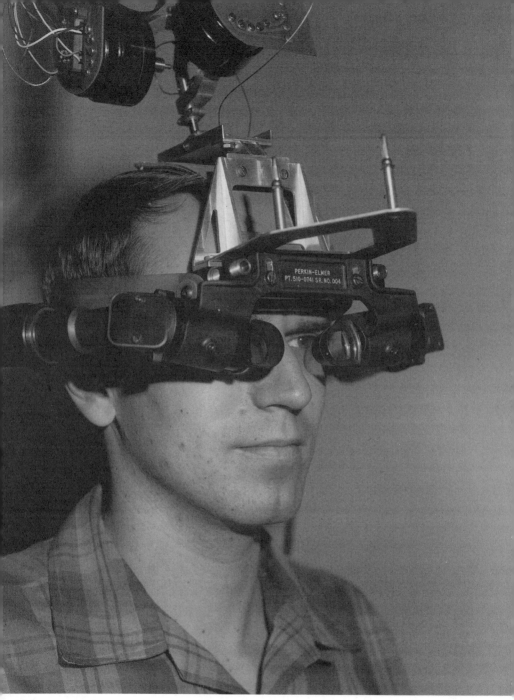

One of Ivan Sutherland's students tests out the head-mounted display Sutherland built in the 1960s. The two prisms in front of the student's eyes reflect computer images from cylindrical cathode-ray tubes.　(University of Utah/Evans & Sutherland Computer Corp.)

puters themselves were chunky, gray behemoths that took up entire rooms, and were so expensive that only governments and major corporations could afford them. People programmed these computers using punch cards, strips of thin cardboard containing patterns of holes that formed a code computers could read. Results were usually printed out on teletypes, electronic typewriters wired into the computer, and were often in a different code that only computer experts could decipher.

Sutherland's HMDs were fairly primitive at first; they displayed only simple forms such as wire-frame boxes. But Sutherland's invention marked the first major step toward the computer technology that would become known as virtual reality.

What Is Virtual Reality?

"Virtual reality" is a shorthand way of referring to a combination of high-speed computers, advanced programming techniques, and interactive devices that makes it seem as if the computer user has stepped into another world—a world constructed of computer data. The data can appear in almost any form: a lamp that can be moved around a room; two molecules that can be combined to form a new drug; even a disembodied hand flying through an ocean of suspended bubbles. But virtual reality systems do not depend on visual trickery alone. Some systems add sound to the images; for example, making the sound of a simulated fountain louder as the user "walks" toward it. In other systems, users control the simulations with electronic gloves that can provide the illusion of texture and solidity.

All these sensations of vision, sound, and touch feed into the brain at once and help create the sense of a three-dimensional "reality." Presenting information as a virtual reality construct makes manipulating data as easy as handling physical objects. By mimicking the way objects look and act in the physical world, virtual reality can help make computers more useful.

Virtual reality, or VR as it is also known, is a technology of the computer age. Its theoretical roots, though, stretch back to discoveries about three-dimensional sight made in the early 1830s. Subsequent developments in photography, in the motion picture industry, and in military technology also contributed to the history of VR. Rather than occurring as the result of a single inventor working toward a single goal, VR came about gradually from the independent work of many scientists, technicians, and designers. In contrast to its slow development, VR has quickly found its way into many differing fields, in part because of the variety of influences that led to its creation.

In architecture, VR techniques allow people to assemble, walk through, and redesign buildings before their real-world construction begins. VR design has already saved corporations millions of dollars that might have been spent on costly real-world modifications.

In medicine, VR displays are being used to teach anatomy without requiring students to dissect dead bodies. Surgeons, by using VR techniques, may someday be able to operate on patients hundreds or thousands of miles away. These surgeons would use tools that give the surgeon a feel for how the operation is going, while automated scalpels would do the actual work on the patient. Chemists are already using VR systems to create new drugs and other compounds by manipulating images of molecules and "fitting" them together.

People are developing tools that use VR to help make money and cut the cost of doing business. Financiers examine and manage their investments with interactive three-dimensional displays. Supermarkets use VR to test new store layouts before rearranging their real-world stores. Advertisers have experimented with ways to promote products with VR sales displays. And real estate companies are taking a look at using immersive computer displays to speed house-hunting trips.

Perhaps the biggest use of VR so far, however, is in the entertainment industry, mostly through video games. Instead of simply standing in front of a cabinet and pushing buttons, VR game players take a more active part in the game: they drive battle robots across alien landscapes while sitting inside

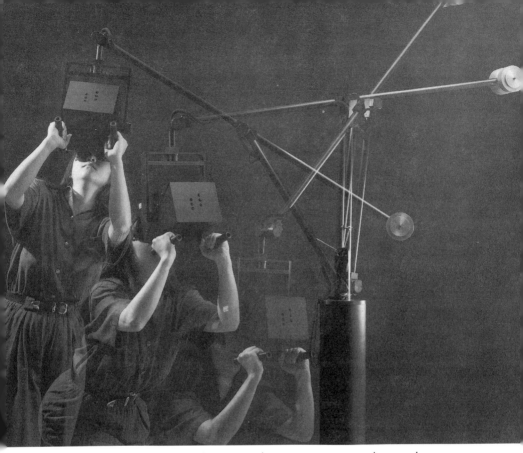

A National Aeronautics and Space Administration researcher explores a virtual environment using the BOOM (Binocular Omni-Orientation Monitor), a VR viewer/controller built by Fakespace Inc.　(Courtesy of National Aeronautics and Space Administration [Ames Research Center])

realistic cockpits, for instance, or they explore undersea fantasy kingdoms.

In the future, virtual reality may play the same role in everyday life that television, telephones, radios, and even the mail play today. Computer experts have already begun putting VR domains onto the World Wide Web, the graphics-oriented subset of the planet-spanning computer Internet. Someday, visiting relatives and friends around the world may be as simple as turning on a computer and stepping into *cyberspace* (a term coined by science fiction writer William Gibson to refer to the perceived world generated by computers). Students may learn history through VR re-creations of past civilizations, or physics by fiddling with VR representations of atoms. As the state of technology advances, VR systems may someday be able to mimic the full range of textures, tastes, and scents of the physical world, as well as its sights and sounds.

How Does Virtual Reality Work?

Virtual reality does not actually take anybody anywhere. VR users do not really merge with the world they perceive, nor do they somehow become part of the computer in the same way that a video monitor or a mouse does. However, the graphics displayed by VR systems are so realistic and the control tools are so easy to use that the user can easily think he or she is in another world. That is the goal of virtual reality.

Tricking the brain into accepting a computerized world as real is a complicated process. Human beings experience the world in three dimensions: height (up and down), width (left and right), and depth (near and far). The key to mimicking the physical world lies in replicating the third dimension, the one that conveys a sense of depth.

For the most part, three-dimensional, or 3-D, perception involves three of the five senses—vision, hearing, and touch. In humans, sight is the most heavily used sense, and it is the sense used most to perceive the 3-D world. People see in three dimensions through the use of *binocular parallax. Binocular* means "two-eyed," and *parallax* refers to the way objects seem to change shape when viewed from different angles. Because the eyes are separated by about 6.5 centimeters (a little over 2.5 inches), each eye registers images at a slightly different angle from the other. These images overlap in the vision-processing area of the brain, which merges the signals coming from each eye into a single three-dimensional picture.

Hearing, the second-most heavily used sense people have, also gives people clues about the three-dimensional world. Most people, upon hearing a noise, can tell from which direction it is coming and roughly judge the distance to its source. Indeed, some people who were born blind or who have lost their sight can navigate through a room by listening to the way sound bounces off objects in their path. Modern VR systems have achieved a great deal of success in mimicking the appearance of 3-D environments by simply combining audio and visual effects. Even some strictly two-dimensional multimedia systems—computers that contain *CD-ROM* (compact disc-read only memory) players, sophisticated sound-effect generators, and high-quality

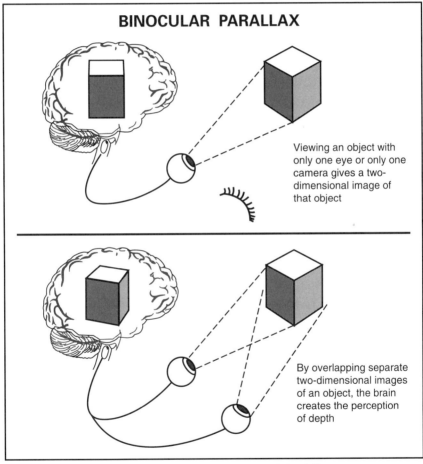

BINOCULAR PARALLAX

Viewing an object with only one eye or only one camera gives a two-dimensional image of that object

By overlapping separate two-dimensional images of an object, the brain creates the perception of depth

The brain perceives depth by combining two slightly different two-dimensional views of objects, a technique called binocular parallax. Some virtual reality systems exploit this phenomenon by giving each eye a different view of virtual environments.

video monitors—are able to give users a feeling of being thrust into the third dimension.

The sense of touch backs up the sight-and-sound world picture with information about weight, shape, hardness, and other details that fix objects in all three dimensions. Touch-oriented, or *haptic*, devices—ones that vibrate, resist movement, or otherwise convey a sense of how objects feel—are becoming as important as visual and audio devices in many computer simulations. (The senses of smell and taste are too hard to replicate with current technology, and are not part of modern VR research.)

A Quick Tour of VR

In its current form, VR can be broken down into three parts. The centerpiece of any VR system is its *reality simulator,* a computer powerful enough to run the complex programs that simulate the real world and fast enough to avoid severe delays that interrupt the illusion of real-world action. Among the components of the reality simulator are *graphics boards,* compilations of *microprocessors* that create the three-dimensional images of the VR worlds; sound processors that can create 3-D sound effects to complement the images; and controllers for the various input and output devices that connect the computer user to the virtual world.

These input/output devices are known as *effectors.* They include HMDs that transmit the reality simulator's 3-D images to the user (and, in some cases, transmit simulated 3-D sound as well); *joysticks,* similar to those used in fighter jets, that are used to manipulate objects displayed in the HMD; *wired gloves* that track where hands are and what they are doing; and other controls that translate human movement into movement of a computerized image in the computer's artificial world.

Finally, there is the computer user, the person who controls what the computer does with its virtual world. VR offers a far more intimate way of interacting with computers than typing in keyboard commands or clicking mouse buttons. In VR, the user

Images created by virtual reality systems are sent to head-mounted displays through graphics boards such as this one.   (Forte Technologies, Inc.)

"wears" the computer—he or she experiences the illusion of directly controlling the work of the computer, of having the computer respond to his or her gestures. And, as computer technology advances, users may indeed one day actually wear their computers, carrying them around as easily as a pair of glasses and a backpack.

Immersing the Audience

This idea of a personally crafted pseudo-reality is not new. Virtual reality came about as a way to satisfy an age-old desire: to visit places or experience events that one would be barred from seeing in person because of distance, lack of money, or physical inability. Central to the goal of virtual reality is the idea of *immersion*, of feeling oneself become part of the experience rather than remaining a passive spectator. For centuries, artists have tried to pull viewers into their works using the phenomenon

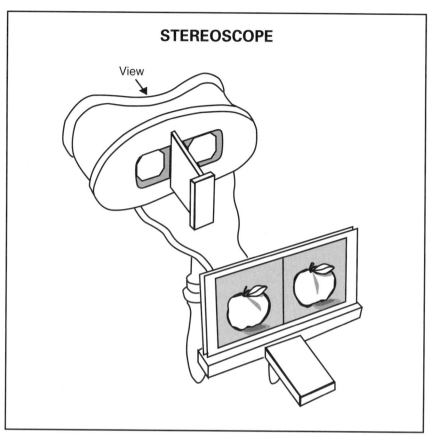

STEREOSCOPE

View

Stereoscopes, which were popular in the 19th and early 20th centuries, presented slightly different views of the same drawing to each eye, creating the optical illusion of three-dimensional sight. Cards displaying the two images were mounted on sliding frames; by adjusting the frames, people could fool their brains into perceiving depth as well as length and width.

of perspective to reproduce three-dimensional scenes in two-dimensional paintings. Because things that are far away look smaller than they do close up, perspective painters combine large and small figures to give the illusion of depth. Yet paintings do not have any true depth to them—they remain two-dimensional representations of a three-dimensional world.

In 1833, British physicist and inventor Sir Charles Wheatstone made use of binocular parallax in a parlor toy called a *stereoscope*. Wheatstone's stereoscope was a simple wooden framework, mounted on a handle, that a viewer could hold in front of his or her face. Two cards showing slightly different views of the same drawing were held in slots on each side of the viewer's head. Two small mirrors angling out from the viewer's nose reflected the cards' images into the viewer's eyes. As the brain merged the two images into one, the viewer suddenly saw the drawing spring to life—not moving, but seeming to pop into three dimensions. Sir David Brewster, another British inventor, improved upon Wheatstone's device in 1844. Brewster put both views on the same card and mounted the card on a movable slide that helped focus the image in front of the viewer's face. He also placed a half-lens in front of each eye to make sure the images would properly blend. By sliding the card back and forth, each viewer could position it at the distance that gave him or her the best 3-D illusion.

This type of stereoscope became immensely popular around the world in the last half of the 19th century and the first few decades of the 20th century. Photographs replaced drawn or painted illustrations, and stereoscope companies used special cameras to create the 3-D illusion. A photographer would set up his camera on a special tripod, take a picture, then move the camera sideways on a built-in rail and take the second picture. (Stereoscopic viewers later found new life in the View-Master, a binocular-shaped stereoscopic viewer that used tiny photographic slides mounted on circles of cardboard.) But the pictures the stereoscope showed did not move and made no sound. While the stereoscope gave visual depth, it offered little else in the way of reproducing reality.

Immersion has also been a central goal of the motion picture industry, which has long sought ways to make moviegoers feel as if they are inside the movies, not just watching them. When motion pictures first came out in the 1890s and early 1900s, the illusion of immersion was not hard to attain. Early movies were of poor quality compared to today's. The pictures were black-and-white and grainy, had no sound, and were beamed by noisy projectors onto screens the size of a bedsheet.

The audiences of the time were not very technologically sophisticated, though. Some customers ran screaming from the theater, afraid of being run over by oncoming horsemen or being shot by bandits whose revolvers seemed to be aimed right at them.

Sound came to the movies in the 1920s, adding to the realism of the stories. Soon after, elaborate special effects heightened the impact of many movies, from war stories to horror films, bringing the audience even farther into the picture. Then, after World War II, the sudden mass appeal of television began drawing audiences away from the theaters. Moviemakers tried a number of gimmicks to keep attendance levels up, including one method that brought the third dimension of depth onto the flat surface of the movie screen.

The three-dimensional experiment was one of the most innovative gambles in the history of motion pictures, primarily because moviemakers could make films using only two-dimensional footage. Fortunately, the illusion of 3-D could be created with a 2-D film, since light waves vibrate in many different directions. The direction in which a beam of light vibrates is called its *polarity*. Light from the sun and from electric bulbs vibrates in many directions at once—left and right, up and down, diagonally, and so forth. Special filters called *polarizers* pass light rays of one polarity and block all others.

Using polarizers and a few other devices attached to their cameras, filmmakers recorded two different polarities of each scene onto the same film. While watching the finished movie, audiences wore special glasses that had separately polarized lenses over each eye. Each eye saw only one polarity of the movie; the brain blended the two images, creating the 3-D effect. (Actually, the effect was more like watching cardboard cutouts move around inside a large box, but it was still impressive.)

A noble experiment, 3-D was too expensive (and many 3-D movies too poorly made) for the technique to last. Although a few companies made attempts to bring it back over the next three decades, 3-D as a cinematic experience essentially died out in the mid-1950s. Ironically, though, it was an innovative Hollywood filmmaker in the 1950s who came closest to creating what might have been the first stage of virtual reality.

Entertaining the Senses

Morton Heilig started working on movies in the early 1950s, around the beginning of the motion picture industry's fling with Cinerama. Cinerama was an extreme-wide-angle filming technique that employed three cameras to shoot each scene and three projectors to show the movie on a huge, curved movie screen. Enthralled with the way Cinerama seemed to surround the audience with the movie, Heilig had an idea of creating an even more personal experience. He wanted to engage all the senses, to entertain the audience with the feel and smell of the story, as well as with the story's sights and sounds. He first attempted to find a way to present these physical sensations to large movie theater audiences, but soon realized that the expense involved made this grand scheme impracticable. He then concentrated on immersing just one person in an all-encompassing display as a means of both demonstrating his idea and earning enough money to develop it further.

By 1960, after six years of work, Heilig had developed two separate devices for presenting three-dimensional simulations of reality. One device, which he patented in 1960, was like the old stereoscopic viewers of the late 19th and early 20th centuries. It combined a three-dimensional slide viewer with stereo headphones and a perfume spray to entertain users with synchronized sights, sounds, and smells. Moreover, this display was portable—it was designed to be worn like a mask, using a brace that went around the user's head. Heilig envisioned replacing the slide viewer with miniature TV screens once technological advances made the substitution possible, creating a three-dimensional, head-mounted TV set.

Unfortunately, while Heilig's prototypical head-mounted display was unique—it earned its inventor a U.S. patent—it did not capture the interest of either the television or the motion picture industries. In addition to his personal viewer design, however, Heilig had put together a one-person arcade ride called the Sensorama. The ride featured a plastic bucket seat mounted in front of a periscope-like display that contained a small 3-D movie screen, stereo speakers, fans, and, as in his stereo headset, a device for reproducing odors. The Sensorama featured a number of scenarios, including a motorcycle ride through New York City. This part of the display came complete with the sensations of bouncing over potholes, hearing traffic pass by on each side, feeling the wind against the rider's face, and smelling food from restaurants.

Unfortunately, like the personal viewer, Sensorama proved unworkable in the real world. While Heilig did sell a few of these machines, they proved unable to withstand the stress of daily arcade use. Breakdowns were frequent and eventually led the arcade owners to abandon these troublesome machines. The experience itself was passive: Users were simply along for the ride, unable to interact with or have any effect on the display. Unable to interest anyone in the entertainment industry in helping him improve his machine, Heilig eventually had to shelve his dreams of an all-encompassing movie.

Morton Heilig's head-mounted television display and Sensorama turned out to be classic examples of ideas that came before their time. Even though the ideas were revolutionary, the revolution they promised was apparent to few people aside from their creator. Moviemakers concentrated on techniques that made 2-D films seem larger than life, later adding advanced recording methods that improved the quality of movie sound. For the most part, the entertainment industry gave up on trying to cross the boundary between two-dimensional displays and the three-dimensional world. But over the next few decades, the knowledge about how to trick people into seeing 3-D images on 2-D screens would come in handy to scientists working in the computer industry.

2
$$\overline{\vee}$$

THE PATH TO VIRTUAL REALITY

*V*irtual reality was created in a number of different steps taken at different times. Two early steps on the path were the discovery of binocular parallax and the invention of the stereoscope in the 19th century. Two crucial steps in the 20th century were the development of computer technology—in particular, the development of computer graphics—and the development of military flight simulators.

A New Way to Control Computers

Around 1963, the time Morton Heilig finally gave up on his all-encompassing displays, a young computer scientist named Ivan Sutherland was conducting ground-breaking research in computer graphics at the Massachusetts Institute of Technology (MIT). At that time, computer graphics—the combined art and science of creating and displaying images on a computer screen—was mostly an unheard-of application. Sutherland almost single-handedly created the field, itself an integral factor of virtual reality, while trying to make computers easier for people to use.

Sutherland started his work in order to take advantage of radical changes in computer design that came about in the early 1960s. A computer is really nothing more than a box containing wires and electronic switches that send electrons through thousands of circuits. Computers manage and display data by rapidly opening and closing switches to change the patterns of the circuits. In modern computers (those built after 1970), these wires and switches are printed on or etched into silicon wafers. (Silicon wafers are round, flat plates of silicon, a material that quickly dissipates heat. Printing computer circuits on a base layer of silicon helps keep the circuits from burning out.) The metal from which the wires and switches are created is layered on top of the silicon wafers, making the components an integral part of the circuit pattern—thus the term *integrated circuit.*

Integrated circuits were the result of decades-long developments in computer technology. The world's first true electronic computer, the ENIAC (short for Electronic Numerical Integrator and Calculator), was switched on at the University of Pennsylvania in 1945. This computer, and those that followed for most of the next 15 years, were controlled mainly by vacuum tubes. Vacuum tubes are airless glass tubes that contain one or more electric wires. In early computers, they acted as switches and allowed the computer to do its work. Vacuum tubes were also used for other electronic devices besides computers: For decades, vacuum tubes controlled radios, radar displays, and television sets.

Vacuum tubes were not very efficient: They used a lot of power, gave off huge amounts of heat, and burned out frequently. When even one of the thousands of tubes in a computer burned out, the entire machine shut down, forcing technicians to spend hours looking for the faulty tube. Vacuum tubes were also bulky, and vacuum tube computers took up whole rooms or even floors of buildings. All of these factors made early computers slow and able to handle only simple mathematical tasks. Even so, these computers could handle these simple tasks far faster than could a room full of people. (Before these vacuum tube-based electronic brains were invented, the word "computer" referred to a person who calculated information by hand. Human computers were widely used by insurance and accounting firms to calculate profits, losses, and insurance rates; by government census bureaus to add up population figures; and by the military to figure out standardized artillery tables.)

Vacuum tubes were succeeded by *transistors*—devices made of small, solid blocks of materials called *semiconductors*. Electricity flows through transistors, but at varying rates depending on the chemical makeup of the semiconductors. Transistors were created in 1948 by three researchers at Bell Laboratories—William Shockley, Walter Brattain, and John Bardeen—who sought a sturdy replacement for vacuum tubes. The three men succeeded. Transistors are smaller than vacuum tubes, use less energy, and are far less vulnerable to damage. Eliminating the bulky, fragile vacuum tubes led to the creation of smaller, more powerful, and less expensive computers. It did not eliminate another major problem, though—making computers easier for people to use.

Easier Interactions with Early Computers

Even with the adoption of transistors in the early 1960s, working with computers was time-consuming, complicated, and somewhat mystical to all but those who actually told the computers what to do. Computers were programmed by trained operators using punch cards—large slips of stiff paper perforated by patterns of holes that contained data ranging from accounting tables to fingerprint records. Some computers presented the results of their calculations on a second set of punch cards, which had to be put through another machine to be decoded. Other computers printed their results on electronic typewriters—but the results were often of little help, since they were in a code that only programmers could read. Thus, computers were extremely user-*un*friendly: Unless a person was one of the special few who knew how computers worked, that person could not use computers.

Ivan Sutherland's goal was to cut through this complicated process and to create a way for anyone, not just those with special training, to use computers. The first interactive system Sutherland came up with at MIT was called Sketchpad. Sketchpad, which opened the door to the development of modern computer graphics, used a light-emitting pen and a keyboard to draw simple designs on a *cathode-ray tube*. (*Cathode-ray tube*, or *CRT*, is the proper name for the glass bottle that forms the display screen on television sets and computer monitors.) For its time, Sketchpad was a remarkable application of computing knowledge. Sketchpad showed that data of almost any type, not just drawings, could be altered and saved in the computer for later use. More important, Sketchpad proved that people could use computers without having to know how to program them. By doing all their work on a computer screen, users did not need to carry around bundles of punch cards for each function they wanted the computer to perform.

Other researchers had been doing work much like Sutherland's. Some of the most important work was done by an engineer named Douglas Engelbart. Engelbart had worked on ways to improve radar displays for the U.S. Navy. Like Sutherland, Engelbart thought that video monitors could be used to both display and control data. In 1968, after more than a decade of research at a number of government-sponsored laboratories in the San Francisco Bay area, Engelbart gave a demonstration of three revolutionary breakthroughs. First, he used a pointing device he called a *mouse*. Second, with the mouse he selected and moved words on a computer's monitor screen. Third, the display used little computer-generated pictures, or *icons*, to represent various codes and commands. These features, which Engelbart developed in 1968, later became commonplace in millions of computers. These features also pointed the way to the development of other human-computer interaction tools, including the effectors used in modern VR systems.

"The Ultimate Display"

The success Sutherland had with the Sketchpad, and his knowledge of the work other researchers were doing, convinced him that computers could be made to interact more naturally with their human users. But the methods of displaying and controlling information that were being developed, his included, still bothered him.

The process people used to interact with computers—what became known as the human-computer interface—was still a matter of humans having to adapt themselves to the unnatural mechanics of the computer. Why not create computers that were designed to accommodate themselves to the way *humans* worked? Sutherland wondered. In 1965, he wrote an article called "The Ultimate Display," in which he proposed creating an immersive computer display that people could use the same way they interacted with the real world. He stated that such a display could also give people "a chance to gain familiarity with concepts not realizable in the physical world," such as mathematical or scientific theories.

Using his article as a guideline, Sutherland went on to build a prototype of his "ultimate display," starting it at MIT and then moving on to complete it at the University of Utah. Sutherland's prototype was the ceiling-supported, head-mounted display described at the beginning of Chapter One, which created three-dimensional wire-frame images that seemed to float in midair. Because the device hung from its motion-tracking support rod, it was nicknamed the Sword of Damocles, after an ancient legend of a Greek nobleman who was forced to sit under

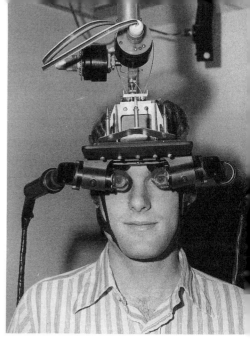

The Sword of Damocles (shown here at the University of Utah) was the first head-mounted display ever built to render computer-generated graphics. It was also one of the most cumbersome HMDs ever built: Its users had to strap themselves into it for the display's 3-D effect to work.
(Courtesy University of Utah/Evans & Sutherland Computer Corp.)

a sword that was suspended by a single hair. Sutherland finished work on the Sword of Damocles in 1968, which seems to have been a good year for computer technology. It was the same year that Engelbart unveiled his mouse and icons.

Simulating Flight

The Sword of Damocles head-mounted display demonstrated that it was possible to present computer data in a form most people would recognize. Unfortunately, the display was expensive, awkward, and extremely limited in the types of images it could show. The best the HMD could do was project wire-frame boxes in midair. Even with the HMD's drawbacks, though, many people understood that the range of its functions would improve as computer technology in general improved. In particular, the display attracted the attention of the U.S. military. The ability to create computerized stand-ins for physical displays, such as those on aircraft, promised a solution to a problem facing fighter pilots. The technologically advanced airplanes being built were so complicated, they were going beyond the pilots' ability to fly them safely and carry out their missions.

With their radar displays, flight data gauges, weapons controls, and other devices, modern fighter jets were forcing pilots to choose from too many options. Pilots were having to find and operate too many controls to keep their planes in the air, out of harm's way, and able to strike at enemy air and ground targets. The military needed a better way for pilots to control their planes. And new pilots needed a comparable method for safely learning how to operate their planes before taking to the skies. A graphics-based airplane control system seemed to be the answer.

Reproducing the physical sensations of flight was nothing new to the flying services. In 1929, a man who designed player pianos and pipe organs, Edwin Link, unveiled a new invention, a training aid that taught student pilots the mechanics of flight. The simulator was a realistic mockup of an airplane cockpit mounted on a platform that tilted in response to the actions of the pilot. Link's simulator also reproduced such phenomena as air turbulence and in-flight stalls. Unlike modern simulators, though, the Link Trainer was an "instruments only" device. On some versions, a hood shaped like the canopy of a real airplane isolated the trainee from the surrounding classroom. The only outside information came from an instructor who monitored each session from a desk near the trainer.

The Link Trainer found enthusiastic customers in the U.S. Army Air Corps (the predecessor to the U.S. Air Force) and in the U.S. Navy's aviation division. The great air battles of World War I had provided one crucial bit of knowledge for fighter pilots—if a pilot survived his first five dogfights, he could reasonably expect to survive a war. The problem was that many pilots got into their first dogfights while they were still figuring out how their aircraft worked. Using simulators, flight instructors could speed up the time it took for pilots to get used to their planes. That way, their students could use more of their real flight time practicing combat maneuvers. This knowledge, in turn, gave many pilots the edge they needed to live through their initial dogfights.

Early fighter simulators featured just the rudimentary aspects of flight, allowing students to learn only the mechanics of

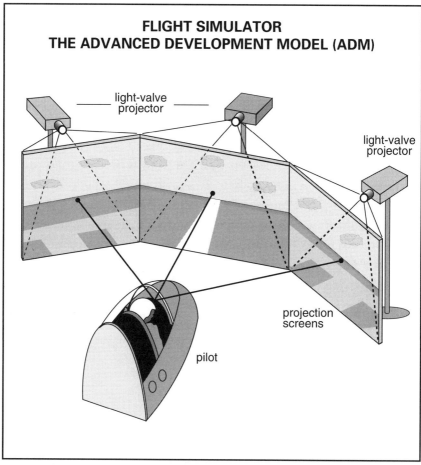

FLIGHT SIMULATOR
THE ADVANCED DEVELOPMENT MODEL (ADM)

light-valve projector

light-valve projector

projection screens

pilot

Many flight simulators—such as this one, developed by the General Electric Company in 1972—surround cockpit mock-ups with computerized environments displayed on rear-projection screens. Other models heighten the simulation using cockpits that tilt in response to the pilot's actions.

how the various controls worked and to experience the general effect they had on the airplane. Students had to wait until they were actually flying through clouds or over hostile terrain to get accustomed to those situations. Later, other companies developed more advanced simulators that produced more accurate simulations. For example, during World War II, films taken from the windows of real airplanes were projected onto small screens surrounding the simulator's cockpit. These films gave pilots a better illusion of flight, but had the drawback of not being able to respond to the pilot's actions. After the war, however, the technology of televised images progressed far enough that simulators could incorporate images from video cameras that "flew" over model airfields and countrysides as the student pilot controlled the simulator.

As with the old Link Trainer, simulators allowed novice pilots to gain basic experience without risking their lives or damaging airplanes worth thousands, and eventually millions, of dollars. As the technology became more sophisticated, the flying services started to use flight simulators to evaluate and hone experienced pilots' skills. But these simulators had their limits. They provided a narrow range of airspace—the largest models simulated only 6 square miles—and were not able to reproduce the extreme high-speed, high-energy maneuvers associated with midair dogfights or air-to-ground attack runs.

Moreover, the simulators were very expensive. Because each airplane in the nation's military had its own unique layout—from cockpit design to aerobatics—each had to have its own unique simulator to reproduce these variables, which added to the cost. Each simulator cost as much as a couple of its real-world counterparts (though cheaper than the cost of a few *real* wrecked airplanes). And when a particular type of airplane became obsolete and left service, the simulator had to be thrown away. This technological "fact of life" became even more of a problem in the 1960s, when, because of the use of microcircuitry and on-board computers, pilots needed simulators that could help them keep pace with their aircraft.

"Darth Vader" in the Cockpit

One way to train pilots to deal with information overload is to expose them to it in simulated flight and combat. By the early 1970s, computers were powerful enough for the military to consider using computer graphics in flight simulators. Various flying services around the world started developing systems that combined cockpit mockups with computer graphics. One such system, built for the U.S. Navy by General Electric Co., surrounded a fighter cockpit with three large screens. Special projectors placed behind these screens projected images of the sky, the sea, and enemy airplanes. This system and others like it went on to become standard tools of military flight simulation.

U.S. Air Force researchers thought of another way to deal with the problem pilots faced. In flight simulators and real airplanes, pilots had to deal with too many dials, displays, and switches. The solution, the Air Force thought, was to eliminate the physical displays and instead give the pilots a simplified, all-inclusive computer display, similar to the one Ivan Sutherland had developed. In the late 1970s, Thomas Furness III, himself an Air Force veteran and an expert in engineering, began creating such a display at Wright-Patterson Air Force Base in Ohio. Furness had spent years working on ways to improve simulator technology, was well acquainted with Sutherland's three-dimensional display, and was eager to adapt three-dimensional displays to a real-world application. What he came up with in 1982, the Visually Coupled Airborne Systems Simulator (VCASS), was far more advanced than the Sword of Damocles. It featured a huge, bug-eyed helmet that contained a pair of high-resolution computer display screens, a stereophonic sound system, and a microphone that allowed pilots to give spoken commands to the computer that was running the simulation. The simulator's helmet monitored a magnetic field that was generated by a nearby transmitter to determine which way the pilot moved his head. Based on these measurements, the computer changed the scene being displayed to match what the pilot would see in real life.

The images displayed by the helmet were fairly basic, yet gave the pilots who wore it enough information to control the simulated airplane and to complete the simulated mission. The landscape over which the pilot "flew" was a simple two-color checkerboard. Colored triangles, boxes, and cylinders represented friendly and hostile airplanes, buildings, and enemy radar envelopes. In the foreground, an airplane-shaped space contained a handful of gauges that monitored fuel level, speed, and other necessary information. Pictures of missiles and bombs indicated which weapons systems were armed and which were on standby.

The VCASS caught the attention of the Air Force officers who were assigned to evaluate it, not in the least part because of its unusual look. The helmet, with its huge oval display screens and insectoid appearance, looked like the one worn by villain Darth Vader in the movie *Star Wars*, which had been released a few years before. But the "Darth Vader" helmet also earned the respect of the Air Force, because of the true-to-life nature of its seemingly simplistic display. The Air Force asked Furness to develop an even better version of the VCASS, a program called the SuperCockpit. At the same time, a group of NASA researchers, hearing about the success of VCASS, decided to combine it with a number of other innovative computer devices to create a new type of engineering workspace. This work would lead to a revolution in how computers presented information.

3
∇
SIMULATING REALITY

Most of the pieces of the virtual reality puzzle had come into being by the early 1980s. Integrated circuits and microprocessors led to the creation of computers that were thousands of times more powerful than those available just 10 years before. VCASS demonstrated the possibility of a wearable computer interface, and other researchers had developed tools in the quest for more user-friendly forms of human-computer interaction.

For one thing, people were trying to create a way to "touch" computer data. At the University of North Carolina at Chapel Hill, a team led by Dr. Frederick Brooks had been working on a way to study chemistry using *force-feedback* simulations. Force-feedback devices use motors to resist or push back against movement from their operators. By varying the amount of resistance or opposing force the motors generate, these devices can create the impression that the user is moving or handling physical objects.

Brooks's work focused on simulating the forces that hold molecules together or cause them to fly apart. One of his most ambitious projects, called GROPE II, used a ceiling-mounted, motorized hand grip to handle computer-graphics building blocks. Unfortunately, Brooks developed GROPE II in the early 1970s, a time when computers still did not have very much power. The ability to stack on-screen building blocks was a respectable achievement for its time, but it was a far cry from being able to reproduce the complex effects of molecular chemistry. But Brooks still thought that GROPE would be a valuable computer interface tool once computers in general had advanced far enough. So he decided to work on other areas of human-computer interaction, putting off further work on GROPE until computer technology caught up.

Putting People in Artificial Realities

Computer researchers and inventors tried other methods of physically manipulating data in the 1970s. Toward the beginning of the decade, a computer scientist and artist named Myron Krueger learned of the work being done with Sword of Damocles-style HMDs. He wondered why people should have to go to that much trouble to work with computers. Why not, he speculated, make computers that watch and respond to humans? Krueger had already experimented with this type of human-computer interaction. From 1969 to 1974, he had built and maintained a pair of computerized artistic environments, GLOWFLOW and METAPLAY, that were displayed at the University of Wisconsin at Madison. In these exhibits, pressure-sensitive floor monitors allowed computers to respond to visitors' movements. The GLOWFLOW computers reacted with sound effects and displays of colored lights. Later, META-PLAY's computers surrounded video images of its visitors with different types of graphics displays.

In 1974, Krueger decided to concentrate on having computers respond solely to the movements of a user's image in an on-screen computer graphics environment. To this end, he put together a system that projected the user's silhouette onto a large video screen. Using the video image, the computer monitored what the user did and changed the display around the image according to how he or she moved. One option this system provided was a sort of finger-painting routine. By extending his or her index finger, the user could draw colored lines all over the video screen. Erasing the design was a matter of simply spreading his or her hand wide open.

This system, which Krueger named VIDEOPLACE, was one of the first examples of what Krueger himself called *artificial reality (AR)*. He envisioned AR as a computer environment that responded to its user directly, rather than through any special bit of clothing. By simply placing the user's image in a computer display, the computer would provide the user with all that he or she needed to control the computer. AR would be a more natural, intuitive interface.

Another attempt at this type of projected computer reality was the "Put That There" system developed in the mid-1970s at the MIT Media Lab. This system's unusual name came from the spoken-word command its developers used most often. A user would sit in front of the system's display screen, which might, for example, display the image of a ship floating on an ocean. Pointing to the ship, the user would say, "Put that." Pointing to another area of the ocean, the user would say, "There," at which the computer would move the image of the ship to its new location.

Two devices made this interaction possible. The first device was a voice monitor the Media Lab researchers created that allowed the computer to recognize spoken commands. The computer could understand a limited number of words—*put, that,* and *there* were about as much as the device could handle—but it was enough for the system to work. Indeed, this device was one of the first successful voice-recognition peripherals ever used in a computer.

The second device was made by a company called Polhemus Navigation Systems. The device was a position sensor about the size of a couple of sugar cubes that could be stuck on the back of the user's hand. Two of these devices were used, along with a magnetic field generator placed near the user's chair. These devices sensed the relative strength or weakness of the field as the user's hand moved within it. One sensor would be closer to the source of the field and would receive a stronger signal. The "Put That There" system combined the signals from both sensors and calculated the position of the user's hand.

Remaking Reality at NASA

Myron Krueger's artificial reality, Thomas Furness's VCASS, the magnetic tracker used in "Put That There," and the desire to manipulate computer data by hand were all fated to come together around 1985. In the early 1980s, video games were starting to become truly popular, personal electronics such as radios were becoming smaller, and NASA scientists were trying to find better ways to evaluate data. One scientist in particular, Michael McGreevy of NASA's Ames Research Center in California was searching for a way to examine three-dimensional objects using computers.

NASA scientists have always been able to come up with unique ways to display data. In the 1960s, NASA sent Surveyor, an unmanned probe, to the moon to send back images in preparation for the upcoming Apollo missions. To get a "lander's-eye view" of the moon, NASA scientists glued the images the Surveyor sent back to the inside of a hollow sphere that had a hole at the bottom. By standing with their heads inside the sphere, they could see a view of the moon as it looked from the Surveyor's landing site.

But what they had was a two-dimensional view of a three-dimensional environment. Up through the early 1980s, there seemed to be no way to replicate three-dimensional environments aside from building full-scale dioramas. Then McGreevy heard about VCASS and the work Thomas Furness had done with three-dimensional computer graphics. McGreevy was intrigued; he thought he could adapt such a system to a host of engineering, design, and exploration projects at Ames Research Center. The only problem was that the helmet Furness created cost more than one million dollars to build. NASA did not have that kind of money to spend on experimental computer displays.

So McGreevy and his colleagues did what engineers have always done when confronted with an impossibility: They worked around it. The personal electronics boom of the 1980s had yielded one extremely interesting bit of technology—a pint-sized television set that featured a 2-inch-square *liquid-crystal display* (LCD) instead of a cathode-ray tube. One of the reasons the "Darth Vader" helmet was so expensive was that it used cutting-edge CRT technology to create extremely clear color images. The black-and-white LCD screens did not give as sharp a picture—their images were made up of tiny dots—but the whole TV set cost only a few hundred dollars.

McGreevy's team decided in 1984 to create a display that might not be as clear, but would be far less expensive. They bought a pair of the hand-held TV sets, removed the screens, and wired them into what looked like a scuba mask connected to a pair of computer graphics boards. A set of special wide-angle lenses in the mask called LEEP Optics, made by Massachusetts-based LEEP Systems Inc., made the images easier to see. The team also attached a Polhemus magnetic position sensor to the mask to allow the computer to track which way the mask pointed. When they finished assembling these pieces, McGreevy and his colleagues had a three-dimensional computer graphics viewer that cost only $2,000.

McGreevy dubbed this new display VIVED, short for Virtual Visual Environment Display. Like Sutherland's Sword of Damocles and Furness's VCASS helmet, VIVED tricked the user's brain into perceiving a computer display as a three-dimensional world. One of the first environments it displayed was an air-traffic control simulation in which wire-frame airplanes floated above a plane made up of a square grid. While wearing the VIVED HMD, observers could "walk" around each airplane, inspecting it from all sides. Because VIVED was so inexpensive compared to other displays, it received a great deal of interest from university researchers, computer manufacturers, and others who realized the benefits of having a three-dimensional computer display.

But VIVED, as far as McGreevy's group was concerned, was still a work in progress. As impressive as it was, it had a number of drawbacks. The displayed objects did not move; there was no way to interact with them, to shift them around or to change their design. Looking at the airplanes was like looking at a sculpture locked inside a glass cabinet. The design team needed to find a way to improve the display.

A New View of Computer Data

At the same time that the NASA researchers were developing VIVED, two video game programmers were trying to build an air guitar that actually made music. Jaron Lanier and Thomas Zimmerman were colleagues at the Atari Research Center in Sunnyvale, California, a town near Stanford University. Atari was one of the world's major video game manufacturers and used the center's staff to stay on top of the market. Zimmerman had been working on a control glove that would turn a computer into a music synthesizer. Each finger of the glove was rigged with a small, flexible tube that carried light from tiny lamps to light-sensing *photoreceptors*. As the wearer bent his or her fingers, the amount of light that reached the photoreceptor changed and varied the signal that the sensor sent to the computer. The computer thus measured how far each fnger bent and responded with the sound a guitar would make as its strings were strummed.

Lanier, who shared Zimmerman's interest in music, also saw Zimmerman's glove as a potential computer programming tool for people who were not professional programmers. Lanier was working on a system that used symbols to represent computer programming codes. With a properly rigged wired glove, he thought, people could grab these symbols and link them like beads on a string. Lanier suggested that Zimmerman attach a position tracker to the back of the glove to let computers track where it moved, as well as how far its fingers bent. The two men decided to develop the glove on their own and left Atari in 1983. Using money Lanier had earned for designing an extremely popular game called Moondust, the programmers started their own firm, VPL Research. They improved the flex sensors on Zimmerman's glove by using *optical fibers* rather than flexible tubes to conduct light. They also added the magnetic tracker that Lanier had suggested. When they finished, they announced the availability of their new product, dubbed the DataGlove.

One of the first people to buy a DataGlove was Scott Fisher, another former Atari Research programmer who had gone to work at Ames Research Center with McGreevy's VIVED group. Fisher saw that adding the DataGlove would give VIVED the interactive dimension that its creators desired. He sought to expand VIVED even further by adding a spoken-word command system and three-dimensional sound. Voice-recognition software was already available, having been used in such projects as the MIT Media Lab's "Put That There" system. Three-dimensional sound was a little more difficult. Simply adding a stereophonic sound system to the HMD would not work. While stereo speakers can move music and sound effects from left to right, they do so in what amounts to a flat plane. They do not give the effect of sounds originating from an object and staying with that object as it moves around.

Fortunately for Fisher, it was possible by 1985 to create three-dimensional-sound simulators that could enhance the VIVED display. Crystal River Engineering, a California company that produced computer sound devices, developed a system that wrapped sounds around the user and added the illusion of depth. The VIVED team incorporated the device, which Crystal River named the Convolvotron, into its system in 1987.

With the addition of sound effects, spoken-word commands, and the ability to manipulate virtual worlds, VIVED was no longer just a visual display. It was a self-contained workstation that people could use far more easily than they could type codes on keyboards while looking at two-dimensional TV screens. More important, the new system caused a shift in the way people thought about how humans could interact with computers. The

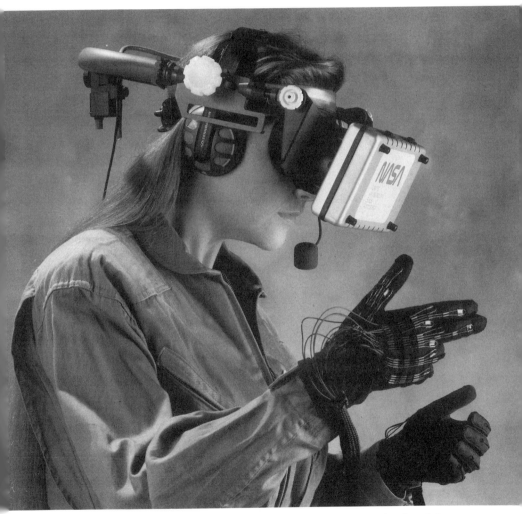

The Virtual Interactive Environment Workstation (VIEW) was the first fully functional virtual reality display in history. It paired VIVED's stereoscopic HMD with other effectors that thrust the user into a self-contained virtual world. (Courtesy National Aeronautics and Space Administration [Ames Research Center])

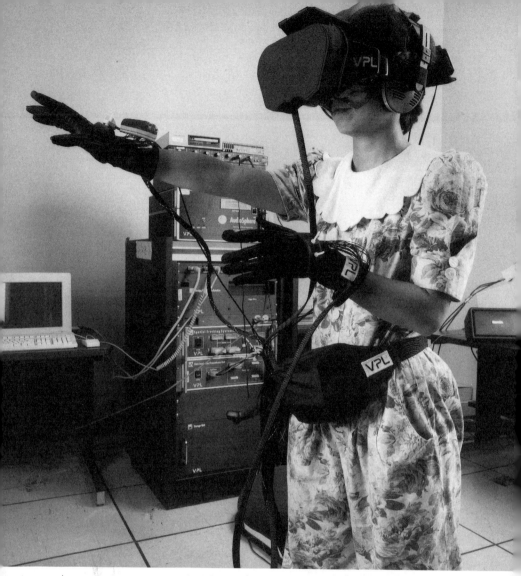

A computer scientist at NASA's Johnson Space Center gives VIEW a try. The tangle of wires and cables sprouting from the various effectors she wears links her to the virtual environment created by VIEW's reality simulator.   (Courtesy National Aeronautics and Space Administration [Johnson Space Center])

system needed a new name to reflect this technological advance and its accompanying shift in thinking. Thus it was christened the Virtual Interactive Environment Workstation (VIEW).

VIEW was as much a revolution in adaptability as it was a revolution in technology. People who saw it realized they could use VIEW for any task, as long as it could be represented as a *virtual environment*. It was not a perfect system, though—even in its final form, VIEW left much to be desired. For one thing, its graphics displays were very primitive. At first, VIEW could display only wire-frame objects, at a level of resolution so poor that one researcher said a person whose vision was that bad in real life would be declared legally blind. VIEW also took a long time playing "catch up" with its users: Quickly turning one's head started a series of stuttering environment shifts in the visual display. More than anything, this lag time hurt the sense of immersion VIEW created.

These drawbacks were more than balanced by VIEW's two main advantages: It was cheap, and it worked. The entire VIEW hardware suite cost less than $10,000, a significant savings over VCASS's million-dollar HMD. The system could be applied to a host of projects, from the original VIVED air-traffic simulation to a simulation of an astronaut maneuvering back to a space shuttle. And despite the grainy, fuzzy images that the LCD screens provided, VIEW *did* create a believable, if not flawless, sense of immersion.

Naming the Future of Computing

Virtual reality officially arrived with the development of VIEW. At the time, though, nobody really knew how popular it might become. There were questions about whether this new technology could be reproduced cheaply enough for other people to buy and use it. There was even a brief time when nobody knew exactly what to *call* it. Should it be called "artificial reality," the term Myron Krueger had used for more than a decade to refer to his immersive environments? Would calling it "virtual environment technology (VET)" be more accurate? The term *virtual reality* was not immediately associated with VIEW and its component computer tools. In fact, the term did not exist until Jaron Lanier came up with it in 1988 to refer to RB2, VPL's Reality

Built for Two VR system, which was based on an improved version of VIEW.

RB2, the world's first commercially produced VR system, ran off an Apple Macintosh computer. The Macintosh controlled two other computers designed by Silicon Graphics, a company that made highly advanced graphics-oriented computers. It came with one or two sets of DataGloves and one or two EyePhones, VPL's version of the 3-D head-mounted display created for VIEW. Later, VPL developed a full-body version of the DataGlove called, appropriately, the DataSuit.

As with all new technologies, RB2 had many drawbacks. One of these drawbacks was its price: it cost more than $400,000 for two people to share the virtual reality experience. (A one-person version cost a mere $225,000.) It also shared many of the image-quality and body-tracking problems of the VIEW system. However, it showed people around the world that the technology worked and that its abilities could be adapted to their needs. Soon, researchers and entrepreneurs in the United States and abroad began developing their own methods of mimicking reality. Virtual reality had arrived, and computer users who saw it wanted to become part of the experience.

4
THE TOOLS OF VR

*W*e experience the physical world through the five senses of sight, sound, touch, smell, and taste. But the organs that perceive these senses do not create our three-dimensional worldview by themselves. Instead, our brains take and combine this information, blending it to give us our view of the solid, physical world.

Mimicking the physical world requires equipment that does more than just act like highly advanced video games. For virtual environments to be believable, they have to incorporate visual, audio, and physical cues similar to those people come across in the everyday world. To successfully immerse their users in the experience, virtual environments must also be as easy to manipulate and as responsive to the movements of their users as the real world. Many tools and programming techniques created after VIEW make this successful immersion possible.

Reality in a Box

Just as the brain is the center of the biological system that allows people to perceive the physical world, computers are the center of the electronic system that tricks the brain into perceiving artificial environments. These computers, called *reality simulators* or *reality engines*, make up one side of the virtual reality equation that yields successful immersion. The other side contains the *effectors*, the input and output devices that people use to work with VR. Reality simulators generate and draw, or *render*, highly detailed images of virtual environments, blending in three-dimensional sound effects where needed. They calculate any touch-related, or *tactile*, effects present in the virtual environment, and rapidly change how the environment looks or behaves in response to the user's actions.

The basic makeup of reality simulators is roughly the same as that of mass-market personal computers, such as the IBM-based or Apple computer systems found in homes and schools around the world. Some of the effectors discussed later in this chapter can be attached to personal computers for basic levels of virtual reality. Advanced VR systems, though, demand much more computational power than that available from standard home computers.

Reality simulators have to be powerful to create even simple virtual environments. A virtual environment's complexity depends on the number of *polygons* that make up the visual display. A polygon is a closed two-dimensional shape with three or more sides, such as a triangle or a rectangle. (Strictly speaking, a circle is not a polygon, as it is a single line curved around on itself.) All landscapes and objects in VR are made up of polygons stuck next to and on top of each other. Even round objects, such as balls or columns, are made up of small polygons attached at very small angles.

Computers use up a lot of memory rendering the thousands of polygons that make up a typical virtual environment. To keep up with a user's actions and provide a realistic world image, a reality simulator has to redraw the environment at least 30 times a second: A slower *refresh rate* causes the display to jerk as the user moves around or alters the environment. Adding sound effects and providing for user interaction place even greater burdens on the system.

Of course, there are ways to ease the burden. Plotting surfaces such as the position of each brick in a wall, for example, is a time- and memory-consuming task. Instead, VR systems use *texture maps*, small computerized "photographs" of surfaces that can be pasted onto virtual structures as needed. A texture map uses far less memory than does a custom rendering, freeing up resources for other tasks.

But reality simulators can do their job only when given effectors that capitalize on their abilities. These effectors can be broken down into four groups: Those that monitor the user as he or she moves, those that let the user see what is happening, those that let the user hear what is happening, and those that let the user manipulate and feel objects in the virtual environment.

Trackers: Where in the (Virtual) World Are You?

For a virtual world to be of any use, its participants have to be able to find out where they are and what they are doing. This is where *trackers* come in—devices that translate a person's real-world movements into data the reality simulator can use to repeat these movements in the virtual world.

The best trackers are those that offer *six-degree-of-freedom* (*6DOF*) movement. Computer graphics displays are organized along the *Cartesian coordinate* system, which divides space into three *axes*: the X axis, which tracks left-right movement; the Y axis, which tracks up-down movement; and the Z axis, which tracks forward-backward movement. Things can move along these axes or spin around them. Each type of movement is considered a separate degree of freedom. A 6DOF device monitors and responds to any movement in any of the three Cartesian axes. In contrast, a *three-degree-of-freedom* (*3DOF*) device monitors along these axes—for example, the movement of a user's

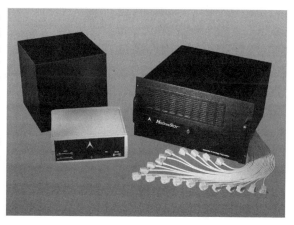

Motion trackers, such as this magnetic tracker system developed by Ascension Technology Corp., let VR systems place their users within virtual environments. (Image Courtesy of Ascension Technology Corporation © 1996)

hand forward and down—but does not register spinning moves, such as the user turning his or her hand upside down.

There are five types of trackers being used in VR systems right now:

Magnetic Trackers   This tracker is the type used in the VCASS/SuperCockpit helmet and the NASA VIEW projects. There are three parts to this system—a small magnetic field generator, a series of up to 20 small magnetic sensors, and a control box that receives data from the sensors and determines their position in the magnetic field. Magnetic tracking is the easiest and most economical method of tracking movement, and thus the one most commonly used in VR systems.

Sonic Trackers   Like magnetic trackers, sonic trackers use body-mounted sensors to pick up signals generated by a fixed source. In this case, the sensors are tiny microphones mounted in multiples of three that pick up ultrasonic pulses sent out by three *transducers*, devices that change electric pulses into sound waves. The control box calculates position and movement based on how long it takes for the microphones to pick up each transducer's signal.

Gyroscopic or Inertial Trackers   These trackers use very small gyroscopes to tell which way the user is tilting his or her head, hands, or body. Inertial trackers are not all that common in current VR systems, because they are not really six-degree-of freedom devices. They measure only changes in orientation, not changes in position: For example, they can tell if a person moves his or her head left or right, but not if that person walks across a room.

Mechanical Trackers These are similar to Ivan Sutherland's Sword of Damocles display, which used a pivoting metal post to track the direction in which the person wearing the HMD was looking. Most mechanical trackers can be used only if the user sits or stands in one place. The most versatile of the mechanically tracked displays are the Binocular Omni-Orientation Monitor (BOOM) made by Fakespace Inc., and the Virtual Reality Spacewalk/Orbiter, made by LEEP Systems Inc.

Visual Trackers This system uses video monitors to track light-emitting diodes (LEDs) or special targets placed on the user, usually on a head-mounted display. These systems are very expensive, so they are used only in highly advanced and highly expensive systems, such as flight simulators.

Virtual Visualization

People generally get most of their information about the world through their eyes. The other four senses mainly serve to clarify or reinforce the signals that the eyes send to the brain. Sight plays an important role in how we deal with the physical world. Most of the work done in virtual reality and many of the tools of VR revolve around re-creating visual cues.

As mentioned in Chapter One, mimicking three-dimensional, or *stereoscopic*, sight is a matter of presenting slightly different views of an image to each eye. There are a number of ways that VR systems make use of this effect, including:

Liquid-Crystal Head-Mounted Displays Basically, this is the same type of device that Jaron Lanier's VPL created for NASA's VIEW system. Most HMDs use separate liquid-crystal displays for each eye, combined with LEEP Optics or other systems that reduce the strain of focusing. Each screen

Some head-mounted displays, such as General Reality's CyberEye HMD, are designed with a flip-up screen that allows users to take a break during extended VR sessions. (Courtesy General Reality Company)

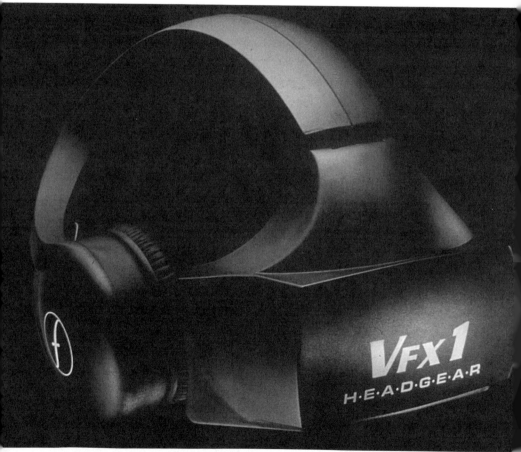

HMDs such as Forte Technologies' VFX1 Headgear are being used in a wide range of commercial, industrial, and scientific applications. (Courtesy Virtuality USA)

measures a couple of inches across and, in most HMDs, connects to a separate graphics board in the computer.

Some HMDs, especially those in less expensive systems or in systems that get a lot of use, have only one screen connected to a single graphics board. This *monoscopic*, or "single-viewed," display does not give the same sense of immersion as a stereoscopic display, but often gives participants a sufficient sense of presence.

In the past few years, another variation of the standard HMD has developed a growing popularity. Rather than placing the display screen directly in front of the user's eyes, it holds the display over the user's eyes horizontally and reflects the image using a pair of partially reflective prisms. This way, HMD makers can eliminate heavier optics. One company that made this type of HMD, Virtual i-O of Seattle, Washington, offered its "i-glasses" line with a detachable visor. Users thus had the choice of totally isolating themselves in their virtual environments or of being able to see the real world around them while working in VR.

Cathode-Ray Tube Head-Mounted Displays This type is much like the Sword of Damocles display that Ivan Sutherland built at the University of Utah. A cathode-ray tube hangs on each side of the user's head, with the display screen pointing forward. A combination of mirrors and lenses reflects the image from the CRT into the user's eyes. HMDs that use cathode-ray tubes give a sharper, clearer picture than do most LCD screens. The better picture does have its price: CRTs are much heavier, far more expensive, and much riskier to use, because they place fairly powerful electric currents next to the user's head.

3-D Glasses Sometimes it is either too expensive or too impracticable to use fully immersive HMDs for three-dimensional displays. In such cases, it is possible to create 3-D images with 2-D computer monitors, much as filmmakers of the 1950s created them on movie screens. There are three ways to do this. The first two involve using glasses with either differently colored or differently polarized lenses. The third method uses electronic "shutter glasses" that rapidly block each eye's view of the display.

The first two methods are roughly the same as those used for 3-D movies. The VR participant wears glasses with red and blue filters or with differently polarized filters over each eye. The VR system renders two images on the monitor at the same time. Each filter blocks out one of the images, giving each eye a separate view to send to the brain. Combined in the visual cortex, the two views yield a seemingly three-dimensional image.

The third method is to rapidly (at least 30 times each second) display alternating left-eye/right-eye views and block the opposite eye in synch with the screen. The glasses used with this method feature a type of liquid-crystal lens that either lets all light through or shuts out all light, like a shutter on a window. Shutter glasses usually have their own batteries, and thus are heavier than red-blue and polarized-filter glasses. They also provide a little more desk clutter, connecting with a wire to a circuit board in the computer that coordinates the shutter effect with the on-screen display.

Other Methods   There have been attempts to create displays that mimic the look of the physical world without using headsets, glasses, or any other cumbersome device. One of the more interesting of these displays places a large liquid-crystal display in front of a series of narrow light panels. The LCD screen displays the left-eye and right-eye images at different angles, switching rapidly between the two to prevent each eye from seeing the opposite image. This *autostereoscopic*, or self-contained 3-D, method has one severe drawback: The illusion of depth takes place only if the user is looking directly at the screen. Any movement beyond a very narrow limit destroys the illusion.

The most successful of the nonobtrusive 3-D displays is one used by advanced Air Force flight simulators and by some VR video game companies. This system uses a series of lenses and computer graphics tricks to fool the eyes into focusing beyond the surface of the computer screen. This arrangement gives an illusion of depth similar to that offered by HMDs or shutter glasses, but with much clearer pictures.

Three-Dimensional Sound

People hear in three dimensions, much as they see in three dimensions, by overlapping two separate sets of signals. Our ears detect *sound waves*, which are nothing more than vibrations that travel through the air. The ability to hear *spatial sound*—to tell the direction from which sounds are coming—comes from the difference in the way each ear captures a particular set of sound waves. For example, imagine walking down a sidewalk when a nearby car blows out a tire. Three things happen. First, the sound of the blowout reaches the ear closer to the car a split second before it gets to the other ear. Though sound waves travel at roughly 1,088 miles per hour at sea level (and a little slower at higher elevations), human beings can perceive lags of as little as 70 microseconds, or 70 millionths of 1 second. This time lag is called the *interaural* ("between the ears") *time difference.*

At the same time, the sound waves strike the closer ear more forcefully than they hit the farther ear. Thus, the closer ear, which points toward the car, hears a louder version of the blowout than does the farther ear, which points away from the car. Because volume depends on a sound wave's *amplitude*—the amount of disturbance a sound wave causes in the air—the difference in volume is called the *interaural amplitude difference.*

Finally, each ear hears a different *frequency*, or range of tones, coming from the blowout. The difference depends on how much sound reflects from nearby walls, the street, and other objects. It also depends on how the sound waves bend as they travel around the listener's head to the farther ear, an effect referred to as the "head-related transfer function." The brain takes all these variables and combines them to determine from which direction the sound of the blowout came.

All these factors—amplitude, time delay, differences in frequency—make creating sounds for a virtual environment more difficult than simply sticking a stereo system onto a big-screen television. For one thing, the sense of hearing is far less forgiving of mistakes and delays than is the sense of sight. The eyes and the visual cortex fill in the gaps when vision is interrupted. This ability, called *persistence of vision*, explains why people can watch a movie's rapid succession of still photos and perceive a continuous, smooth flow of action. But the ears are more sensitive to interruptions, even those as little as 70 microseconds long. Even slight breaks or quavers in a virtual sound display can spoil the sense of immersion. Right now, virtual reality systems get around the problem by playing prerecorded sound files rather than by generating each sound as it is needed.

Just as special circuit boards can adjust the visual displays for each eye, audio circuit boards can adjust the playback for each ear. For example, a person wearing a sight-and-sound HMD and standing in the middle of a virtual room might hear the sound of a radio off to one side. When that person turns to look at the radio, the sound will follow his or her head around until it seems to be coming from in front of his or her head, where the radio is.

Touching Objects in Thin Air: Manipulation Devices

Being able to move around, see, and hear in virtual environments is of little use if you cannot interact with the display. The whole point of virtual reality is to work with computer data as easily as working with physical objects, which involves touching and handling them. There are three general types of devices that allow people to manipulate objects in virtual environments: wired gloves, controllers that look and act much like point-and-click mice, and *haptic* ("touch-related") devices that give an idea of what virtual objects feel like.

Wired Gloves VPL's DataGlove set the standard for most manipulation devices that have been devised during VR's brief history. Gloves wired with fiber optic, electric, or mechanical sensors measure how hands and fingers flex, and send this data to the reality simulator. The reality simulator uses the data to position the user's hand in the virtual environment and to monitor how the user is interacting with virtual objects.

Wired gloves are widely used because of their convenience. They are easy to put on, it is simple to learn how to use them, and they offer a fairly inexpensive and compact way to interact with computers. They can also be combined with magnetic or sonic trackers to monitor how the user's hand moves in physical and virtual space. Controlling software lets the computer determine when the user's hand grasps an object or is blocked by an impermeable surface, such as a wall.

3-D Mice and Other Beasties The mouse, with the point-and-click ability it affords for controlling computer programs, did more to personalize the desktop computer than did any other peripheral. (A *peripheral* is any device that attaches to the computer and helps a person use the computer. Video monitors, keyboards, and printers are other types of peripherals.) Similar tools are being used in virtual reality systems along with or instead of wired gloves. One such controller looks like a

Wired gloves such as General Reality's 5th Glove, seen here, allow VR users to manipulate objects in virtual environments as if they were in the physical world. In this glove, as in many others, fiber optic sensors measure how far the fingers bend. Other devices on the back of the glove track the hand's position in space. (Courtesy General Reality Company)

conventional mouse, but uses an ultrasonic tracking system to convert from standard use to three-dimensional navigation.

Force balls are somewhat similar to 3-D mice. A typical force ball is a hollow sphere covered with rubber and mounted on a curved platform that is connected to the VR computer. Unlike a track ball, the force ball itself does not move. But pushing, pulling, and twisting the ball activates strain sensors mounted inside the sphere. The sensors translate the force they measure into six-degree-of-freedom movement in the virtual world. A series of buttons mounted on the force ball's platform allows users to grab and move objects or change positions in the virtual world.

Wands are a third type of manipulator that do very well in some virtual environments. These can look like remote TV controls, flattened flashlights, or jet fighter joysticks without a base. Whatever their shape, wands usually contain built-in magnetic, sonic, or gyroscopic trackers, and feature a few buttons used to interact with the environment.

Haptics   Some controllers, including a few types of wired gloves, give their users a sense of how the virtual environments feel. These controllers are generally called *haptic*, or touch-sensation, devices. Right now, there are two classes of haptic devices. The first type relies on skin stimulation techniques to trigger touch receptors. Such triggers include air sacs that inflate over sensitive areas of the fingers and the palm, pins that press lightly on the tips of the fingers, and vibrators that change speed to indicate hard or soft surfaces.

The other class of haptic device uses the method of *force-feedback*, or pushing against the muscles rather than stimulating the skin's receptor cells. Historically, most force-feedback manipulators have been large enough to cover the whole arm or hand. They have also been difficult to put on and take off, and awkward to use. Most forced the user to stay in one place for a long time or contort his or her limbs in uncomfortable ways. However, in 1990, Thomas Massie, a student working at the MIT Artificial Intelligence Laboratory, developed a revolution-

The PHANToM uses a fairly simple interface to create realistic force-feedback haptic effects for virtual worlds.   (Provided by SensAble Technologies, Inc, Cambridge, MA)

ary way to present force-feedback in a small, easily used unit. Called the PHANToM (*P*ersonal *HA*ptic I*NT*erface *M*echanism), the device features a motorized arm that ends in a free-moving thimble or other small handle. Motors at the other end of the arm apply varying levels of force in three dimensions, based on the type of surfaces or objects programmed into the virtual environment. Writing with a pencil or pushing a button involves concentrating a force on a single point. Likewise, manipulating virtual objects with the PHANToM involves using a single point—for example, the thimble—to transmit force from the motors to the user's muscles. Essentially, the PHANToM tricks the brain into perceiving the pressure against the muscles as evidence of solid shapes or different textures.

Working in Wide-Open Spaces: Projection-Based VR

Most of the tools described so far—HMDs, wired gloves, and so on—demand that people dress up to work with virtual reality. There are, however, less cumbersome ways to experience virtual environments.

Myron Krueger's goal of artificial reality—projecting interactive computerized environments onto large screens—is still finding applications more than 20 years after he began to work toward it. The Cave Automatic Virtual Environment, or CAVE, is one example of this style of projected VR. Three screens and four color projectors create three walls and the floor of a 10' x 10' x 10' cube in which people can share and interact with three-dimensional virtual worlds. With highly advanced versions of LCD shutter glasses, the CAVE can make virtual objects seem to float in the "real world" space between the display screens. CAVE participants can easily manipulate objects or move around the environment using control wands linked to the computers generating the display.

A simplified version of the CAVE, the ImmersaDesk, reproduces the CAVE effect with just one screen. It was designed as an office-oriented VR display, one that could be used for architectural or mechanical design. Another type of projected VR is being developed at the MIT Media Lab. Called ALIVE, or Artificial Life Interactive Video Environment, it combines video images of the user and his or her room with computer graphics to create a system that responds to a participant's actions. One application of ALIVE, called Smart Room, features a cartoon-like computer graphics dog that can do various tasks and obey commands, including shaking hands with the participant.

The main drawback to these projected VR systems is the amount of space they take up: One could not stash a CAVE system, for example, in a corner of the family room. But these

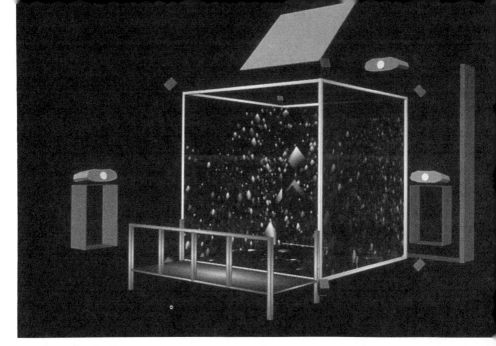

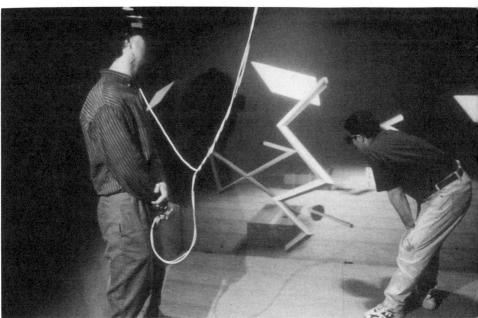

The CAVE is one of a number of systems that offer an alternative to HMD-and-glove-style virtual reality. These systems can all trace their conceptual roots back to the work of artificial reality pioneer Myron Krueger.
(© 1992 Alan Millman and Sumit Das, Electronic Visualization Laboratory, University of Illinois at Chicago)   (© 1995 Courtesy of Roberta Dupuis-Devlin, Office of Publication Services, University of Illinois at Chicago)

systems offer a type of effortless group interaction that is harder to achieve with HMD-and-glove systems.

Augmented Reality

Augmented reality is a technology related to virtual reality that uses many of the same tools as do VR systems. Augmented reality differs from virtual reality, in that augmented reality enhances, rather than replaces, one's view of the physical world. In a sense, augmented reality is a return to the Sword of Damocles that Ivan Sutherland created in the 1960s. A typical augmented reality system features transparent optics that reflect computer-generated images into the user's eye. This way, the images appear to overlay real objects in front of the user.

Augmented reality has the potential to become a real benefit to physicians, engineers, and other professionals who do intricate or complex tasks. Using an augmented reality system, an airplane mechanic could project an instruction manual over his or her view of an airplane's engine, with arrows linking portions of diagrams to their real-world counterparts. Physicians could display *x-ray* or *ultrasound* images on their patients as they examined or operated on them. But these applications are a few years away. Right now, augmented reality is in its developmental stage. A number of hurdles still must be overcome, the biggest of which is developing a way to make computers lay images precisely over real-world objects. If this and other problems are solved, mechanics might one day replace physical instruction manuals with a computer display built into a pair of glasses.

5
∇

VIRTUAL
ARCHITECTURE

---

*D*esigning any building is a complicated process involving hours of planning and drawing. Architects have to transform their ideas of how a three-dimensional building should look into two-dimensional blueprints. This task can easily go awry, creating problems that are expensive or even impossible to fix after construction begins. Floor plans that seem to work on paper can turn out to be difficult to build, inconvenient to walk through, or simply ugly when finished.

Architects try to catch these problems before construction begins by building three-dimensional models of the blueprints they create. But these models are too small to let their viewers do anything but imagine what it would be like to stand in the future building. Because these models are small, their viewers can overlook details that are noticeable in a full-size room, such as a door that is too narrow.

Using immersive, interactive virtual environments instead of small-scale physical models would make avoiding these problems easier. Architects and their clients could move around the building and interact with the proposed floor plan. They could open doors and windows, walk up and down staircases, and even (in some cases) check how well the building looks compared to nearby buildings. They could then immediately alter the model to test out any changes. Because the original design would be saved in the computer, the architect could undo any changes that turned out to be unnecessary.

Altering Virtual Office Buildings

Architectural design is a three-stage process. First, the architect comes up with an idea for a building. Next, he or she prepares a model or a drawing of the building, adding such details as plumbing, air-conditioning, and electrical systems. Finally, the architect presents the idea to other people—the architect's clients, other architects, builders—for evaluation. This process feeds back upon itself, as the architect takes the suggestions he or she received on how to improve the design of the building, changes the plans, and resubmits them for further comment.

Virtual reality promises to speed up this process. Using virtual reality tools, an architect will be able to, as one researcher says, "kind of scribble in virtual space just as quickly as he or she can jot down an idea or draw out a napkin sketch." The architect will then be able to expand upon this computerized scribbling, developing full-scale plans and discarding unworkable ideas—without cluttering up his or her workspace with old napkins.

Right now, the most common use of virtual reality in architecture involves taking clients on tours of proposed building designs. One of the earliest examples of virtual architecture was the Sitterson Hall project at the University of North Carolina at Chapel Hill. The university built Sitterson Hall, which houses the UNC computer science department, in the late 1980s. Before construction started, though, some students and

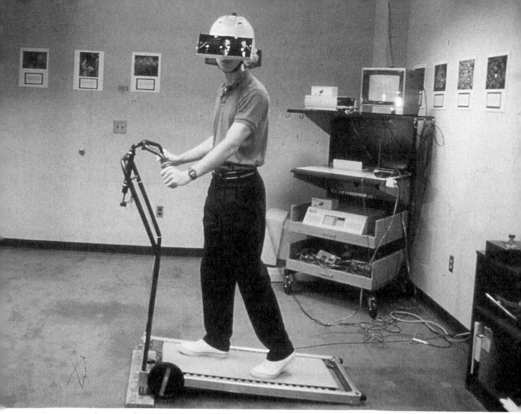

A researcher at the University of North Carolina at Chapel Hill walks through a VR mockup of the planned Sitterson Hall building in the late 1980s. Participants in the early architectural VR experiment used the handlebars on the treadmill to change direction in the computer-generated environment. (Courtesy University of North Carolina at Chapel Hill, Department of Computer Science)

research professors took a copy of the architect's blueprints and created a computer model of the building. They then toured the model using a head-mounted display and an exercise treadmill wired to serve as a sort of human-powered mouse. As the model's "visitors" moved through the virtual building, a sensor on the treadmill told the computer how far the visitors had walked. A movable set of bicycle handlebars let these virtual-world tourists steer themselves anywhere a person could walk in the real building.

Even though the quality of the display was fairly primitive, the overall effect was good enough for the researchers to see where the building's design needed changing. In one case, the building's architects had placed a low wall between a lobby and a hallway to separate the two areas. While examining their VR model, the researchers discovered that the arrangement made the hallway too narrow. The architects were reluctant to change the design until they saw how it looked in the VR mockup. Since the university researchers were right, the architects moved the wall. Now, the discovery that a wall was out of place was not, in itself, remarkable. The remarkable thing was that the researchers discovered the flaw even though the blueprints indicated that the hallway was wide enough. Without the VR model, the building would have gone up as designed, and the researchers would have had to put up with a cramped hallway.

Since the Sitterson Hall walkthrough was created, researchers have improved the techniques used at UNC. Their goal has been to create architectural simulations that are as detailed as a real building, yet as easy to rearrange as a set of building blocks. Researchers at the Human Interface Technology (HIT) Lab at the University of Washington in Seattle developed a set of virtual building blocks that they have been

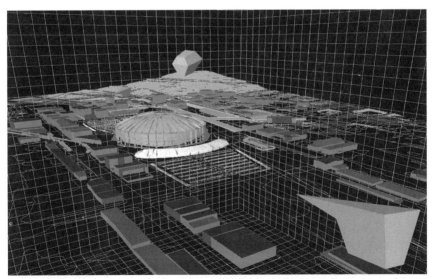

The "Blocksmith" project at the HIT Lab in Seattle was used to create this interactive model of the new stadium being built for the Seattle Mariners. (Courtesy Human Interface Technology Laboratory)

using for a few years. Developed for a program called the Blocksmith, these blocks can be stacked next to and on top of each other, stretched into a variety of shapes, and molded into almost any desired form. Using Blocksmith, HIT Lab researchers have built a number of large 3-D VR models. For one project, they created three-dimensional models for a series of proposed designs for the stadium that will replace Seattle's Kingdome in the 21st century.

Smaller projects also benefit from VR simulations. In Japan, for instance, a custom kitchen manufacturer created a VR design simulator for its main Tokyo showroom. By putting on an HMD and a wired glove, customers could walk through various kitchen designs, turning on faucets and opening cabinet doors. Elsewhere, researchers have used VR to tailor houses and apartments to the unique needs of people who rely on wheelchairs to get around. A program at the Hines Rehabilitation and R&D Center in Chicago used a wheelchair mounted on a special platform to measure where people moved in a virtual home. The participants opened doors, turned lights on and off, and did other tasks using a wired glove. The researchers used the data from these tests to design rooms and place fixtures that were more convenient for wheelchair-bound residents.

Detecting Design Flaws with Virtual Reality

Using virtual reality to design buildings also promises to help architects avoid costly design problems that do not appear until the building goes up. In 1996, a construction firm fought off a lawsuit over a series of leaking roofs in a 64-story office building with the aid of a 3-D computer simulation. The top of the building, Two Prudential Plaza in Chicago, looked like a pyramid made up of four staircases resting against each other. Unfortunately, the individual roofs that made up the staircase allowed rainwater to leak inside and drip through the ceilings of the offices below them. The building's owners sued the company that built the tower, Turner Construction, for the cost of repairing the water damage and fixing the roofs. The owners claimed that the company had not followed the blueprints properly when it put up the roofs.

Turner Construction's owners and lawyers knew that the tower had been built according to the plans. But how could they prove that the original roof design had been flawed? And even more important, how could they convince the jury that the original design's flaws, not sloppy construction, caused the leaks? The best way to do all this seemed to be to take the jury on a tour of the original roofs and compare them to the new roofs that the owners had installed. Turner Construction hired Engineering Applications, a company in Iowa that specialized in engineering simulations, to help prove that the original design had been flawed. Using the original blueprints, Engineering Applications put together a three-dimensional computer simulation showing how the original design let water find its way into the building. The construction company's laywers presented the simulation to the jury on a large, two-dimensional monitor. However, the display was detailed enough for the jurors to understand how the original roof structure worked in three dimensions. Combined with other evidence, this simulation convinced the jury in the lawsuit that the construction company was not to blame for the damage caused by the badly designed roofs.

If a two-dimensional presentation of a three-dimensional model is enough to teach a jury about structural engineering, what could trained architects do with a fully immersive model of a planned building? Many architects and VR researchers think that such a system would let architects head off expensive problems, such as the one that struck Two Prudential Plaza. A fully immersive virtual building tester could also simplify another problem of architecture: making sure that buildings can weather real-world physical phenomena.

Escaping Disaster with VR Design

There are many stresses that can ruin a seemingly well-designed building. On the West Coast of the United States and in other seismically active areas of the world, such as Japan, buildings have to be both strong enough and flexible enough to ride out powerful earthquakes. Heavy winter snows can crush the roofs of homes and stores that are not designed to bear the added weight. Even heavy winds can cause a seemingly sturdy building to sway, shake, or collapse if it is not designed properly. In a virtual environment, architects could throw the stresses of the physical world against their designs and quickly change those designs that fail.

While these types of systems are still a few years off, some systems in use today *are* doing remarkable work. In the United Kingdom, a company that develops evacuation plans is using VR to improve how people flee buildings in an emergency. The company, Colt Virtual Reality, created a virtual environment program that lets researchers study how groups of up to 500 people might react to fires or other mishaps. The program, called VEGAS (short for Virtual Egress Analysis and Simulation), provides virtual evacuees with programmable "personalities" based on studies of how people have reacted to actual disasters.

Using VEGAS simulations, researchers have discovered a number of ways to make it easier for people to leave a room in an emergency. Noticing that a standard door measuring 2.5 feet (74 centimeters) wide lets 120 people through in 1 minute, a Colt VR researcher decided to widen the doorway. After a little experimentation, the researcher found that twice as many people could hurry through a door that was only 8 inches (20 centimeters) wider. However, that was with the computerized people jamming together, getting in each other's way as they fled. A more orderly flow, the researcher thought, might be even better for getting people through the door. This theory held true in the model when the researcher added a railing that pointed out from the doorway. The railing forced the fleeing mob into two lines, resulting in an extra 70 people getting through the door. In the end, the number of simulated evacuees who could get through the door in 1 minute jumped from 120 to more than 300. By expanding beyond simulations involving relatively small groups such as these, Colt VR researchers envision being able to plan evacuations for neighborhoods or whole towns during floods or other disasters.

A Virtually Guaranteed Presentation

Along with its current and potential abilities as a design tool, VR can be an impressive vehicle for swaying clients toward approving an architect's ideas. In one case, VR techniques were used to help bring the 1996 Republican presidential nominations to Southern California.

When the Republican Party began looking for a host city for its national convention, it took bids from such cities as New York, Chicago, New Orleans—and San Diego. Few people thought that San Diego's biggest meeting site, the San Diego Convention Center, could hold all the people expected to attend the nominations. Presidential nominations usually took place in huge convention halls, with floors measured in acres and with ceilings up to 70 feet high. In contrast, the San Diego Convention Center had intentionally been designed as a smaller alternative to these larger halls, which as a result of their size were more expensive to rent. Party officials expected 20,000 to attend the Republican National Convention. The convention center, however, was designed to hold only 12,000 people comfortably.

To show the Republican Party that the convention center was big enough to hold all the delegates, the center officials turned to virtual reality. Specifically, they turned to the San Diego Data Processing Corporation, a nonprofit computing and simulation company owned by the City of San Diego. The convention center created a VR version of the facility as it might look during the nominations. The model included broadcast platforms for the major TV news organizations, suggested seating for the convention delegates, and a stage and speaker's podium based on one used during the Republicans' 1984 convention. (To appeal to the 1996 convention organizers, the display included a still image of former president Ronald Reagan speaking from the podium, and featured signs naming the organizers' home states.) The tour of the proposed convention floor included showing how the convention would look from cameras mounted in various locations and at various heights around the main floor.

Buildings for a Virtual World

There is another way that virtual reality is being combined with the field of architecture, however. Instead of using VR to design buildings for the physical world, some researchers are using VR to design buildings for *virtual* worlds. In other words, instead of using VR *for* architecture, they are using VR *as* architecture.

One researcher who is exploring this alternative use for VR architecture is Dace Campbell, a former graduate student at the HIT Lab in Seattle who became an intern architect at the architecture firm NBBJ and a consultant at the HIT Lab. He and others in his field see a need for designers who can tailor the theories of architecture to the needs of virtual reality. This area of study is commonly known as cyber architecture or liquid architecture, though Campbell prefers to call it by a simpler term: *virtual architecture.*

The greatest need for virtual architecture, as envisioned by Campbell and others, will come from the Internet—mainly from its graphics-heavy subsidiary, the World Wide Web. More people are working in and exploring the Internet than ever before. But working with this globe-spanning network of linked computers today means having to memorize the long strings of letters, numbers, and arcane symbols that make up Internet and Web addresses. The task facing architects is to come up with ways for people to navigate in and interact with the computerized world as easily as they interact in the physical world.

The easiest way to do this, from a user's standpoint, is to use three-dimensional graphics and other sense cues that can act as landmarks for on-line explorers. "Virtual architecture, then," Campbell says, "would serve a similar function (to that of physical architecture), except it's composed of polygons and vertices and texture maps, as opposed to bricks and mortar and steel."

The main difference between virtual architecture and physical architecture will be the lack of constraints on the virtual architect's work. Unless it is programmed into an environment,

Architectural models can be combined with other VR design techniques to form a fully immersive environment. In this illustration, a Swedish mass transit systems manufacturer, Adtranz, has used the dVISE modeling system created by Division Inc., a British VR firm, to construct a virtual urban train station.   (Courtesy Division Inc.)

there is no such thing as gravity in virtual reality. There are no such things as sun, wind, or rain. There are no property lines, building codes, or fire dangers; no worries about budget limits; nor any other physical-world constraints that affect how virtual environments behave. The only limits are the amount of memory in the reality simulator, the speed at which the simulator operates, and the skill of the programmer or programmers involved in building the environment. In virtual reality, buildings do not even need to have front doors.

One of Campbell's projects as a graduate student involved building a gallery of virtual environments that looked more like a space station than a museum. The gallery's entryway was a bridge from nowhere leading into a series of exhibit halls. Each picture in the gallery was a link to a separate virtual environment; visitors could "jump through" the pictures into the environments they displayed. The exhibit halls looked like cubes, half circles, and rectangular slabs standing on end. They stuck out from the overall structure at angles impossible to achieve in the physical world.

This sort of freedom will be the hallmark of virtual architecture. Virtual architects may have to make concessions to people's physical-world expectations (such as establishing a "down" or a "forward" in the virtual environment). Eventually, though, virtual architecture may become an important field of expertise in developing a building's overall look. For example, in the future many people will use their computers for banking rather than wait in line at a physical bank building. A well-designed VR interaction site may one day be as important to a bank as conveniently located branch buildings.

6

SCIENCE AND ENGINEERING WITH VR

*S*cientists observe the physical world and try to explain why it works the way it does. Engineers take what is known about the physical world and use it to create technologies that enhance our lives. Both science and engineering demand the ability to think about how the physical world works and to imagine how it might change. Virtual reality is helping scientists and engineers by giving substance to their ideas.

In a sense, VR came about *because* scientists and engineers wanted to give substance to their ideas. Ivan Sutherland did not build his Sword of Damocles just to make using computers easier; he also wanted to let scientists and mathematicians work in a "mathematical wonderland." He envisioned scientists using his "ultimate display" to watch how the various forces of nature interact, rather than just calculating their effects on a blackboard. Frederick Brooks designed his GROPE project, which gained renewed life with the computer technology advances of the 1980s, as a hands-on tool for customizing chemical reactions. The creators of VCASS, VIVED, and VIEW sought ways to present complicated technical or scientific data in an easily comprehended, easily manipulated form. This scientific and technical heritage still influences most VR applications.

Getting a Feel for Microscopic Worlds

The GROPE project at the University of North Carolina at Chapel Hill was one of the first truly usable scientific applications of VR. Researchers manipulated a computer display using an Argonne Remote Manipulator (ARM), a large remote-control device originally used by nuclear plant workers. Mounted on a post hanging from the ceiling, the ARM transferred workers' hand and arm movements to robotic arms that handled nuclear materials inside shielded workspaces. (*Argonne* refers to Argonne National Laboratory in Illinois, a federally funded research lab that develops and explores the possibilities of cutting-edge technology.)

For GROPE, Frederick Brooks and his colleagues fitted the ARM with a combination of electric motors that turned the manipulator into a force-feedback effector. As computer technology advanced through the 1980s, GROPE was repeatedly modified and given better-quality displays than the ones available during the 1970s, when it was first developed. Before long, researchers were able to juggle computer-generated molecules with the ARM while watching a projected 3-D display. The modified ARM simulated the physical reactions of the molecules by pushing or pulling the user's hand and arm. Real molecules carry slight charges that attract molecules to each other or push them apart, depending on the molecules' chemical makeup. If

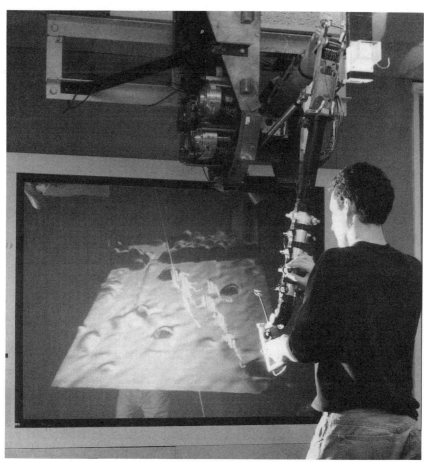

UNC researcher Mike Falvo uses the university's modified ARM to work with the nanoManipulator system. (Courtesy University of North Carolina at Chapel Hill, Department of Computer Science)

the GROPE operator tried to link two virtual molecules that repelled each other, the ARM would suddenly stop moving. If the virtual molecules were attracted to each other, the ARM would pop forward slightly, indicating a successful docking.

GROPE, in its various versions, provided years of good service to the computer scientists and chemists who used it in their experiments. Recently, though, UNC researchers have begun using a different force-feedback device, the PHANToM haptic manipulator developed by Thomas Massie at MIT. Working in virtual environments with the desktop-mounted PHAN-ToM and its single-finger interface is easier than handling the extra mass of the larger, bulkier ARM. (For one thing, researchers can sit down while using the PHANToM.) The smaller device is also less expensive to buy and maintain than is the ARM.

PHANToM has gradually replaced the ARM as the main effector in a number of projects, primarily in UNC's experimental nanoManipulator program. NanoManipulator is an example

In another version of UNC's nanoManipulator, Mike Falvo uses a PHAN-ToM force-feedback device to move objects that are measured on the nanometer scale. The shutter glasses he is wearing turn the image on the computer monitor into a three-dimensional display. (Courtesy University of North Carolina at Chapel Hill, Department of Computer Science)

of how people can use VR to control machines in remote, dangerous, or inaccessible locations. This kind of remote control through virtual reality is called *telerobotics, teleoperation,* or *telepresence.*

NanoManipulator offers scientists the opportunity to work directly in the realm of the very small. Researchers use the system to work with objects that are measured in *nanometers,* distances of one billionth of a meter (.000000039 inch), such as viruses or chemical compounds. Objects this small are made visible by using *scanning probe microscopes.* A scanning probe microscope scans an extremely tiny needle-like probe back and forth over objects placed in the microscope's testing chamber. One type of probe uses a beam of electrons to keep a fixed distance above these objects; another type triggers a motor in the microscope that raises the probe when it touches an obstruction in its path. The microscope creates a video image of the objects over which the probe travels, based on how high the microscope has to lift the probe. By carefully handling the probe, researchers can move objects with the probe's tip or with the electron beam the probe emits.

The nanoManipulator displays the microscope's data in a 3-D virtual environment rendered on a desktop computer monitor. Shutter glasses turn the monitor's flat display into a stereoscopic simulation. Such displays allow scientists to conduct experiments they otherwise could not do. In one project, UNC researchers have studied the tobacco mosaic virus, a major threat to the tobacco crops of the Southeast. Using the nanoManipulator, the researchers have moved single viruses into tiny electric circuits. The ability of a virus to conduct electricity, its *electric potential,* can tell scientists much about the virus' physical and chemical makeup.

The combination of VR and scanning probe microscopes can also be used to handle other materials on the nanometer scale. As a demonstration of the nanoManipulator's dexterity, UNC scientists have nudged tiny particles of gold through gaps in equally tiny gold wires, like athletes kicking soccer balls though solid-gold goals.

Exploring Other Planets via VR

Telepresence may one day let scientists work on other planets as ably as it lets them work in the microscopic world. NASA researcher Larry Li at the Johnson Space Center in Houston has been experimenting with telepresence exploration since 1990. His Dexterous Anthropomorphic Robotic Testbed (DART) pairs a standard VR system with a two-armed robot torso that transmits stereoscopic images with a pair of video cameras. To operate the robot, a user sits in a magnetically tracked chair and dons an HMD and a set of gloves. A reality simulator transmits the user's movements to the robot and displays what the robot's cameras see in the HMD. The user can also control the robot with a few spoken commands that, among other things, lock the robot's arms in place and switch the HMD view to a camera near its right hand.

The DART's design team hopes that the system will one day be used to explore the moon or Mars. Little is known about either planet, despite the manned lunar missions of the 1960s and 1970s and the unmanned exploration of Mars. Using a telepresence system would let scientists directly experience these alien landscapes without the high cost of sending human explorers across the void of space. Tests have shown that the DART would be able to do some of the tasks that human explorers could do. For example, geologists have used the DART to chip off rock samples from small boulders in the Johnson Space Center laboratory.

There would even be an added benefit to conducting long-range explorations such as a mission to Mars. Radio signals travel at the speed of light, a little more than 186,280 miles in one second. Mars's orbit is so far from Earth's, though, that radio signals take anywhere from 8 to 20 minutes to travel between the two planets. This delay would not allow scientists to control a robot in *real time*, to have commands instantly obeyed and to see the robot's actions as they occur. But this apparent drawback could actually be of benefit to Earth-bound

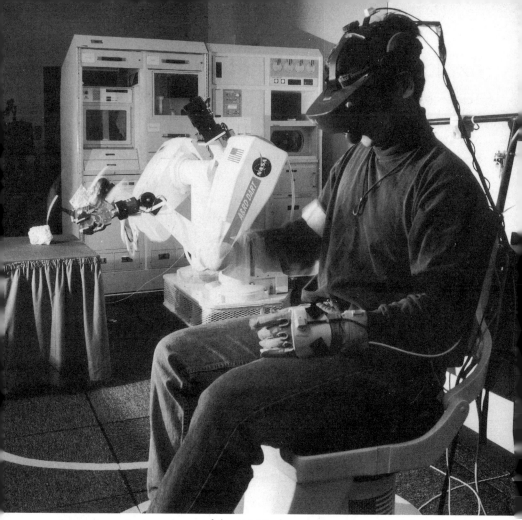

Larry Li, project engineer of the DART, demonstrates how Earth-bound explorers might use a VR-controlled machine to gather rock samples on distant planets. (Courtesy National Aeronautics and Space Administration [Johnson Space Center])

scientists. The robot could transmit enough data about its surroundings for the reality simulator to create a virtual Martian environment. Using their VR effectors, scientists could practice a series of tasks that the robot might perform. Once they decided what the robot should do, the scientists could transmit the appropriate command codes to the robot.

Telepresence is also being explored as a means of safely working in unsafe environments. At Sandia National Laboratories (another high-tech federal government lab) in New Mexico, researchers are working on VR-operated repair vehicles that could navigate through damaged nuclear power or chemical plants. With such a system, human operators could quickly and accurately evaluate the damage while staying away from any radioactive materials or hazardous chemicals. They could then either repair the damage or determine what would need to be done to bring the situation under control. Elsewhere, marine scientists are developing virtual environments to control deep-sea exploration vessels. One such project is taking place at NASA's Ames Research Center. The Telepresence Remotely Operated Vehicle (TROV) uses a virtual environment control system to direct a small submersible. NASA scientists have already used the TROV to explore the sea floor beneath the ice of Antarctica and within the boundaries of Monterey Bay, while controlling the vessel from Ames.

VR and Scientific Visualization

Science is not a haphazard process, but one that follows a fairly straightforward path of investigation called the *scientific method*. The scientific method involves observing a phenomenon; suggesting a *hypothesis*, or an explanation of what causes the phenomenon; conducting experiments to test the hypothesis; and seeing whether the results of the experiments prove or disprove the hypothesis. Finally, for a hypothesis to be considered a valid *theory*, other scientists have to be able to conduct the same experiments and get the same results. Virtual reality systems can help scientists in each of these areas.

Directly observing natural phenomena is not always possible, or, when possible, it is not always convenient. Think of what an astronomer has to do to analyze a supernova (an exploding star). Because supernovas occur in deep space, comparatively few of their effects travel far enough for Earthlings to observe. At most, people on Earth can detect the light the explosion produces; a burst of radio waves, cosmic rays, and a few other types of radiation; and, hundreds or thousands of years later, the immense dust cloud, or *nebula*, that the explosion leaves behind.

Analyzing this information with special (but non-VR) instruments, astronomers can determine the power of the explosion, what type of gases it produced, and even how it affected nearby stars. Combining this information to form a clear, detailed picture of the event can be tricky. Most of the data are presented as two-dimensional graphs, lists of numbers, and computer-colored pictures of the event or of its aftermath. The only three-dimensional image astronomers get is the one they create in their minds' eye.

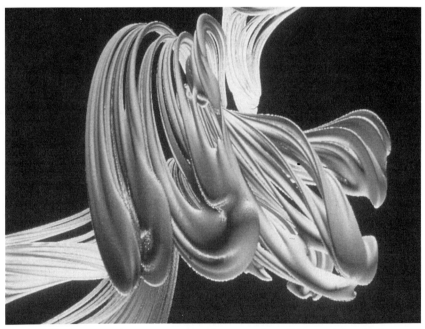

The CAVE also contributes to science by providing 3-D models of advanced mathematical formulas. This image shows a Julia Set, a map of how a complex equation behaves when its results are fed back into itself. Mathematical functions such as these can be accurately visualized only with a 3-D display.   (© 1995 Daniel J. Sandin and Joe Insley, Electronic Visualization Laboratory, and Louis H. Kauffman and Yumei Dang, Department of Mathematics, Statistics and Computer Science, University of Illinois at Chicago)

This problem sparked a project at the University of Illinois at Chicago (UIC) in its Electronic Visualization Laboratory, where the CAVE projected-VR system was created. The supercomputer that controls the CAVE is powerful enough to handle the immense amounts of data required to realistically simulate such details. This project, the Cosmic Worm, uses the CAVE to create 3-D models of how space behaves around supernovas and other cosmic events. Astronomers can travel around and through these models, seeing how the various forces of the explosion interact. Like most other applications of VR, the Cosmic Worm is more of a demonstration project than a fully operational scientific tool. Even so, astronomers who have studied data in the Cosmic Worm say they have achieved a level of understanding they could not have reached any other way.

Running Experiments in Virtual Labs

The CAVE is proving itself as a versatile scientific and engineering research tool in other ways. A team of researchers at UIC and at Wayne State University in Detroit, Michigan, have used the CAVE to build a virtual environment called the SANDBOX, in which scientists can analyze their data or data from other scientists' work. (*SANDBOX* is short for "Scientists Accessing Necessary Data Based On eXperimentation.") In the SANDBOX, a scientist could verify the results of an experiment by recreating it using graphic representations of lab equipment. Conceivably, any experiment could be reenacted, as long as its procedure and results were available in easily accessed computer files, or *databases*. The SANDBOX would also allow the scientist to browse through related databases to retrieve information, or to conduct a rapid search for a specific bit of knowledge.

While the virtual experiment was running, the scientist could display other related data. He or she could review notes written by other researchers, examine maps or photographs taken of real-world locations related to the experiment, even hang graphs of previous experiments on surrounding virtual walls. The scientist could also use more than just the sense of sight to interpret data. The SANDBOX's designers incorporated sound effects into the environment, such as the sound of fluids dripping into beakers in a chemistry lab. The SANDBOX's creators even used unusual sounds to represent some measurements, such as playing the high-pitched buzz of a cicada to represent the average temperature of a series of thermometers. The cicada buzz increases as the temperature rises and grows silent as things cool down.

Blowing in the (Virtual) Wind

Meteorology, the study of weather and the atmosphere, is a field that seems tailor-made for virtual reality applications. Weather is an incredibly complex phenomenon: It combines the effects of air pressure, air temperature, ground temperature, terrain, and a host of other variables.

Researchers at Argonne National Laboratory—where the ARM was created—have been adapting the CAVE to a range of scientific uses. One of their projects uses a CAVE to simulate weather patterns as they develop over an area of the United States. The simulation includes a 3-D terrain map and adjustable controls for air pressure, temperature, and other effects. Any wind generated in the simulation is represented by colored arrows, with the colors changing depending on how fast the wind blows.

The simulation shows where the wind would blow faster, such as over hilltops or through valleys. It also shows differing wind patterns at various layers in the atmosphere. Wind does not blow in a solid mass over the ground; there are many wind streams blowing in different directions at different levels in the atmosphere. If these streams were seen from above, they would seem to crisscross each other like reeds in a woven mat. Researchers studying these virtual weather displays use a control want to travel around the simulation, focusing on high-wind areas or pulling back to get the big picture. They can even track the wind as it blows over the virtual terrain by dropping a computer-generated ribbon that sails through the simulation.

Other researchers at the Argonne lab are adapting the CAVE to control the flow of a different type of stream—a stream of atomic particles traveling through complex electromagnetic fields. Scientists who study radiation and its effects send streams of atomic particles through magnetic field generators called "wigglers"—so named because they wiggle the path of the particles as the particles pass through them. Wiggling the particles causes them to emit short bursts of radiation, such as X rays, which the scientists can use for a range of other experiments. Changing the strength and orientation of the electromagnetic field alters the strength and duration of these bursts of radiation. Using VR to examine how particles wiggle as they go through the fields will give scientists a better feel for how to alter the fields in the real world.

Engineering: Blowing in the (Virtual) Wind, Part II

If science is the discipline that lets us understand how the world works, engineering is the discipline that lets us figure out what to do with it. Just as architects can use VR to test and change building designs, engineers can use—and are using—VR to test and modify tools, machines, and mechanical systems.

Another way that NASA's Ames Research Center has expanded upon VIEW's virtual environment technology is a system called the Virtual Windtunnel. Wind tunnels are structures that vehicle designers use to measure how air flows over and presses on mockups of their designs, and sometimes on prototypes of the vehicles themselves. A wind tunnel looks like a long, smooth-walled corridor with a large fan at one end. The fan's speed, and in some setups the angle of its blades, can be adjusted to create winds from light breezes to full-blown gales. Depending on the size of the model placed inside the wind tunnel, engineers can simulate anything from the effects on a commercial jet flying at 20,000 feet to the air resistance a car meets traveling at 30 miles per hour.

For all their versatility, wind tunnels are expensive to build and run, and the experiments that they are used for take much

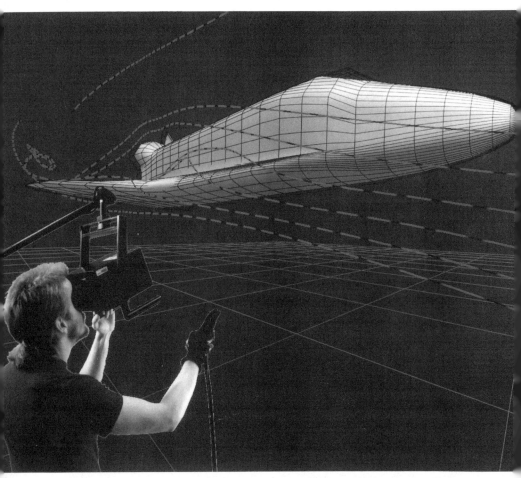

Engineers can use NASA's Virtual Windtunnel to evaluate how well their designs stand up to turbulence in the air. Here, an engineer uses a BOOM display and a wired glove controller to test a virtual space shuttle model.   (Courtesy National Aeronautics and Space Administration)

time to set up. Ames researchers developed the Virtual Windtunnel as an inexpensive and less labor-intensive alternative to physical wind tunnels. The Virtual Windtunnel combines a wired glove, like the VPL Research DataGlove, with a mechanically tracked Fakespace BOOM 3-D display. The system calculates and renders the image of air flowing over a computerized representation of a vehicle, such as a space shuttle. Using the glove, designers can change variables such as airspeed and the angle at which the vehicle moves through the air.

Creating Better Construction Equipment with VR

Another way engineers make use of VR is through *virtual prototyping*. A *prototype* is a practice version of a tool or machine that engineers build to see whether their ideas can stand up to the stresses of real-world use. In a way, a prototype is similar to the physical models architects construct to demonstrate their building ideas. Unlike an architectural display, a mechanical prototype is a working model of the tool, machine, or vehicle the engineer designs.

Virtual prototypes are working models constructed in virtual environments rather than in the real world. Virtual prototyping is an outgrowth of *computer-aided design*, or *CAD*, a sophisticated means of designing three-dimensional objects—from heavy machinery to houses—on two-dimensional computer displays. CAD is itself a type of proto-VR, as it allows a limited amount of interaction with the design. Virtual prototyping can save companies a lot of money by speeding up the time and reducing or eliminating the need to build real-world mockups. At the same time, the ease with which VR objects can be altered means that changes in a design can be made within minutes.

The CAVE environment used to design the 914G incorporated a physical reproduction of the wheel loader's controls. The driver is wearing shutter glasses that allow him to perceive the flat computer graphics as a three-dimensional environment. (Courtesy Kem Ahlers, Manager of University Relations, Caterpillar Inc.)

This method of industrial engineering has been a fact for a couple of years. In the spring of 1995, Caterpillar Inc., a construction equipment maker, began building a newly redesigned model of its popular line of wheel loaders. This particular loader, the 914G, was different from Caterpillar's previous models. Its rear end sloped away from the operator's cab, making it easier to see what was behind the loader, a welcome change from the squared-off boxes of previous models. The loader's shovel and body were also designed to provide fewer visual obstructions as the operator worked in construction sites.

More remarkably, the new model had gone into production in record time. Caterpillar had started redesigning its loader in the fall of 1991. Normally, it can take up to seven years to get a new model ready for production. Testing physical prototypes of the new model takes up most of this time; any flaws in one prototype can be changed and evaluated only by building another prototype or, sometimes, by modifying the first one. The 914G, though, had been prototyped in an early version of the CAVE. The Caterpillar design team controlled a virtual mockup of the wheel loader with a physical mockup of the loader's control cab. Caterpillar engineers and loader operators "drove" the VR machine around a simulated construction site, moving virtual dirt piles and doing other jobs that the real loader would have to do. Testing alternate designs was simpler in VR than in real life. Rather than build a whole new machine, the engineers simply programmed the changes into the CAVE's computer. Prototyping the loader in VR cut the time it took to produce the final version of the loader to a little over three years, saving Caterpillar millions of dollars.

Virtual prototyping provides a faster, less expensive alternative to creating physical test versions of products. Here, Ford Motor Co. uses Division Inc.'s dVISE modeling software to evaluate planned changes in its Bronco sport utility truck.   (Courtesy Division Inc.)

Other companies have learned the benefits of virtual prototyping as well. Automakers including Ford Motor Co., General Motors Corp., and Volvo have used VR to make improvements in a number of cars. Ford, for one, used a design system created by a British VR company, Division Inc., to test planned alterations to its Bronco sport utility truck. Volvo has taken this application one step farther by providing virtual reality simulators to its dealerships as sales tools. Customers can "test drive" a range of cars without leaving the dealer's showroom by simply putting on an HMD and sitting in a mockup of a car's driver seat.

Comfort and Convenience, Courtesy of VR

Virtual prototyping is not limited to simulating the mechanics of a product. It can also account for the comfort and convenience of the people who use that product, be it an automobile or a factory workspace. *Ergonomics*, the art of designing products that are comfortable to use, is a very exacting field. Engineers use body measurements taken from hundreds of people to sculpt equipment controls and build seats and work areas that conform to their human users. Experimenting with ergonomic mockups is a lengthy and expensive process, as is building machinery prototypes. And, as with VR machinery prototypes, adjusting ergonomic layouts in VR can save a great deal of time and money.

To do this, designers use computerized human figures that are rendered at the same scale as the equipment or spaces being designed. These figures can be as simple or as detailed as their users require. Division Inc. incorporates fairly detailed figures it calls "manikins" in its design environments. Designers can place these manikins on a truck's driver seat to see whether there is enough space between the figure's knees and the steering

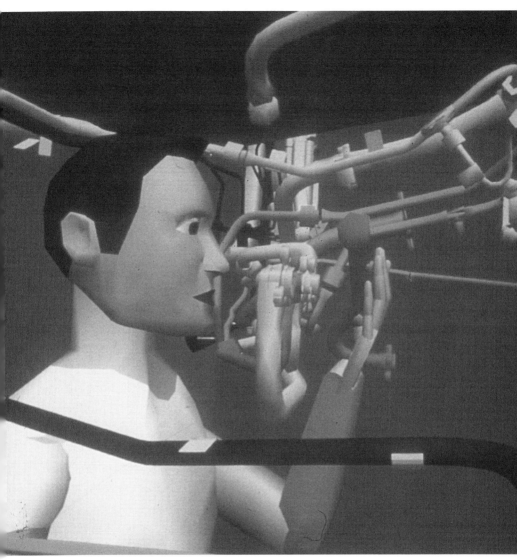

Computer-generated human figures, such as the Division "manikin" shown here, can help engineers design workspaces in which it is easier to move around, and mechanical systems that are less complicated to decipher. (Courtesy Division Inc.)

wheel. These figures can also serve as stand-ins for mechanics as engineers evaluate how easy it is to reach and work on the truck's machinery.

7
$$\overline{\vee}$$

MEDICINE AND VR

Medicine is one area of science that will use virtual reality to directly benefit nonscientists. Even though VR is a still-emerging technology, medical doctors are already finding ways to incorporate it in the work they do. Surgeons are developing virtual reality tools they can use to test out medical procedures before their patients enter the hospital. Physical therapists are using simulations to show people with a range of handicaps how to function ably in the everyday world. Even psychiatrists have been able to use VR to help people confront and overcome their deepest fears in controlled virtual environments. VR gives practitioners in these and other fields the ability to do risky work safely and practice complicated tasks until they gain proficiency.

Medical Training with VR

The human body is an incredibly complex system of organs, blood vessels, muscles, bones, and other conglomerations of living cells. Learning the anatomy of the human body, how all these structures and tissues fit and work together, can be an overwhelming task. Yet medical students have to learn anatomy to understand how to treat the sick. Cutting into the body to heal it is a risky matter, even with the high quality of medical care available today. But surgeons have to be able to apply their skills and knowledge to their patients' maladies. Virtual reality can play an extremely useful role in both these areas.

Much of the difficulty in *learning* anatomy comes from how schools *teach* anatomy. Even though the human body is a three-dimensional structure, medical students learn this structure mainly by studying two-dimensional charts and medical textbook illustrations. Schools do provide human skeletons and physical models of various sections of the body for study, but these resources are too expensive for most students to have their own copy. Skeletons can cost up to $2,500, and a useful model of just part of the upper body can easily cost the same.

Virtual reality's ability to mimic the appearance of three-dimensional structures promises a cheaper and more useful alternative. There are a number of research projects around the

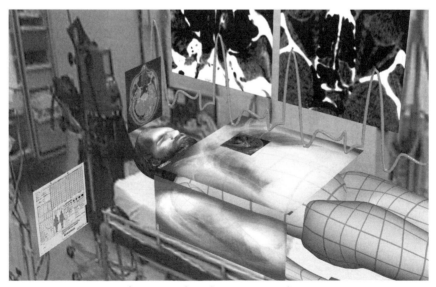

VR environments are being explored as a way to better arrange emergency rooms in hospitals. This image comes from a HIT Lab replica of the trauma center at Harborview Medical Center in Seattle. *(Courtesy HIT Lab)*

world aimed at creating interactive, easily explored models of the human body. One such project at the German National Research Center for Computer Science uses a projected VR system to display a human body for virtual dissection on a tabletop screen. The computer-generated body seems to be lying on top of the screen, much as a real body would lie on an operating table—a useful effect for medical students. Viewing the projection with shutter glasses, the student can peel away layers from the body using a wired glove. He or she can pull bones from the skeleton for closer examination, or grasp the heart to study how it works.

This and other VR dissection methods will be in the experimental stage for a while, offering views of only a portion of the human body's anatomy. Two things will have to happen before people can study full VR models of the body. First, the technology itself will have to improve. The quality of the images will need to progress from the fairly cartoonish figures available today, and reality simulators will have to handle greater amounts of data faster. Also, a fully detailed model of the human body will have to be compiled. The body is too complicated for anyone to mimic it in a virtual environment designed from scratch.

Fortunately, creating a full display from scratch will probably not be necessary. There are a number of databases already available that feature two-dimensional cross-sections of entire human bodies. One of these is the Visible Human database at the University of Colorado School of Medicine, which contains photos of 1 millimeter-wide (.04 inch) cross-sections of human cadavers. This information is already being used in conventional computer programs that teach anatomy. Most of these anatomy tutorials use multimedia techniques—including hypertext and audiovisual presentations—to enhance the 2-D visual display. It should be a fairly straightforward task to create fully immersive virtual environments based on this information; that is, once VR technology is able to handle the extreme amount of detail such an environment would contain.

If such an environment *were* made available, it would solve a number of problems in training physicians. It would, of course, make learning anatomy easier, as students could see how various systems interacted. It would also shorten the time it took for surgeons to develop their abilities. To apply his or her surgical knowledge successfully, a surgeon has to have had at least some experience in operating on the human body. However, practicing on living human bodies is out of the question. Learning to operate on cadavers is a common practice, but dead bodies simply do not act the same way living bodies do when cut open. What is worse, once a cadaver has been "operated" on, there is no way to undo the work and give another surgeon-in-training a fresh start.

This is where virtual reality can make a big difference. Corpseless dissections—especially ones in which a virtual body would be programmed to bleed and otherwise act as would a real, living body—would be as realistic a simulation as could be desired. This method would also be reusable, as the simulation could be reset once a student finished dissecting it. The simulation would also be easier to care for. Cadavers have to be preserved with special chemicals and stored in refrigerated vaults to keep them from decaying. A VR re-creation of a human body, on the other hand, needs only a computer with sufficient storage space.

Preparing for Real Surgery

Eventually, a surgeon-in-training has to start treating real people, a major transition that no surgeon makes alone. Airplane pilots do not fly solo until they have flown a certain number of hours under an instructor's supervision. Likewise, new surgeons do not operate on patients without going through an apprenticeship called a "residency." They first observe and assist experienced surgeons. They then perform operations while experienced surgeons observe them. Only after being certified as competent does a surgeon begin to operate on his or her own.

Each operation is unique, each patient responds to treatment differently, and surgeons need much practice to be able to handle these variables.

Practicing ways to handle ever-changing situations is a task well suited for virtual reality. By feeding details of a patient's condition into a surgical simulator, surgeons could try out a variety of treatments, discarding ones that did not work and correcting any mistakes. In this manner, surgeons could eliminate much of the uncertainty that accompanies any operation. Aside from the software that would control such a simulation, the main need is for a reliable way to simulate the feel of surgery in virtual reality. A number of methods are being developed to replicate this sensation.

Many of the methods that have been studied combine virtual reality with augmented reality. One such project combines a standard HMD-and-glove setup with a rubber or polymer mockup of a human torso. The surgeon uses a scalpel to cut into the physical model while looking at a VR display in the HMD. With proper placement, the HMD's image of the scalpel, the surgeon's hand, and the patient matches the positions of the real-world scalpel, hand, and patient. Unfortunately, methods such as this are a long way from being widely used. The technology is not good enough yet for a reliable overlap of the virtual and physical worlds.

Doing the entire operation in a virtual environment, thus eliminating the need for physical mockups, can solve this problem. Just as UNC researchers were able to move viruses using the force-feedback PHANToM, there are a few projects that use PHANToM force-feedback armatures to perform virtual surgery. One project, developed by PHANToM inventor Thomas Massie, mimics a procedure for probing brain tumors. The procedure, a biopsy, involves sticking a needle through the skull and into the brain until it reaches the tumor. The PHANToM simulation reproduces the feel of a needle poking through the scalp, the skull, and various layers of brain tissue.

Safer Surgery through Simulation

Although surgery involves cutting into the human body, surgeons strive to do the fewest incisions necessary to fix whatever is wrong. In the past few decades, surgeons have begun using *endoscopic* ("inside view") surgery, also known as keyhole surgery, as an alternative to opening up large areas of the body. Making smaller incisions does less damage to the body and ultimately speeds up a patient's recovery time. One of the most well-known forms of keyhole surgery is *arthroscopic* knee surgery (*arthroscopic* means "looking at the joint"), which is often performed on professional athletes. Another common keyhole operation in *laparoscopy*, which involves operating inside the chest or abdomen.

In a laparoscopy, the surgeon inserts his or her instruments into the body through *trocars*, tubes with a one-way gasket on the end that stays outside the body. One of the tools the surgeon uses combines a tiny video camera and optical-fiber lights to send images of the operation to a video monitor. Watching the screen, the surgeon manipulates surgical instruments that are inserted through other trocars. The major drawback to keyhole surgery is that surgeons cannot see exactly what they are doing. They operate on the body by looking at images of the operation site, not by looking at the site itself. This is a hard technique to master, and a surgeon who is learning how to perform these operations can unintentionally hurt a patient. A number of keyhole operations have gone wrong simply because the surgeons could not find the operation site or because they lost track of where their instruments were.

Virtual reality techniques could help surgeons jump past the risks associated with this learning period. For one thing, simulating the procedure could raise the skill levels of new endoscopic surgeons. Two groups in the United Kingdom—Virtual Presence, a VR simulation company, and the North of England Wolfson Centre for Minimally Invasive Therapy in Manchester—have developed such a simulation for laparoscopy. Called MIST VR (short for Minimally Invasive Surgery Training

Virtual reality environments are being developed to help physicians prepare for and carry out complicated surgical procedures. One promising application of surgical VR involves creating computer simulations of endoscopic operations, such as the Virtual Shoulder Arthroscopy model seen here.   (Courtesy Proslovia Clarus)

by Virtual Reality) it reproduces the combination of two- and three-dimensional cues that exist in current keyhole surgery. With MIST VR, students manipulate a three-dimensional surgical environment with two laparoscopic instruments. As the students go through a series of increasingly difficult simulations, experienced surgeons can track how well the students are learning the techniques. Because surgeons coordinate their physical movements with video images in real-world endoscopic operations, they do not need such full-immersion gear as HMDs.

VR in the OR

There is a difference between applying knowledge gained in virtual reality to a real-life operation and using virtual reality as an aid *in* a real-life operation. As good as MIST VR is, it only prepares surgeons to navigate through three-dimensional space by looking at pictures on a two-dimensional monitor. A better system would allow surgeons to look at a three-dimensional image of the operation. It just so happens that some researchers are working on two ways of creating such images.

Augmented reality, as mentioned in Chapter Three, projects computer-generated images over views of the real world. Most of the research being done with augmented reality is designed to help mechanics and technicians build and repair machines. Some augmented reality research, however, focuses on opening a "magic window" in the side of patients on the operating table. One such research project under way at the University of North Carolina at Chapel Hill is aimed at letting surgeons have better control over breast and liver needle biopsies. A needle biopsy involves taking cell samples from a part of the body using a special needle. By analyzing these samples, doctors can gauge the health of the organ from which the cells came. Guiding the biopsy needle to the correct spot is a tricky matter, especially when the doctor performing the biopsy is searching for a small site.

The goal of the UNC project is to combine data from ultrasound, X-ray, or other types of scans and project them over the site of the biopsy to aid the doctor in guiding the needle to the correct site. So far, researchers have been struggling to create a display that is good enough to show the fairly narrow biopsy needle against the surrounding tissue. Once this problem is overcome, though, the system will make the procedure both faster and safer.

Another method being developed immerses the surgeon entirely in a virtual environment while he or she performs an operation. As the surgeon works on the VR patient, a surgical robot reproduces the surgeon's actions on a real patient, possibly in an operating room far from where the surgeon is working. This type of technology in which a human remotely operates a robotic manipulator is called teleoperation, telepresence, or simply telerobotics (also discussed in Chapter Six). Eye surgery

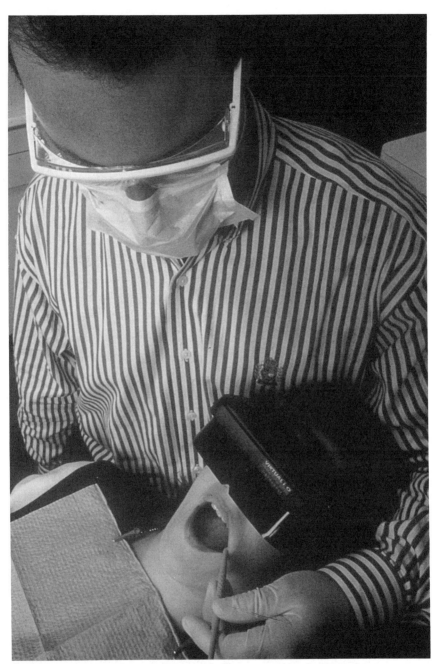

Sometimes keeping a patient's mind off a procedure helps reduce any pain the patient might feel. Here, a set of Virtual i-O's i-glasses is being used to keep a dentist's patient distracted from the work going on in her mouth. (Courtesy Virtual i-O)

is one field in which this method could be applied. An instrumentation scientist working at the Massachusetts Institute of Technology, Ian Hunter, has been working on such a system for a few years. His system combines a stereoscopic display with a control handle that lets an eye surgeon cut into the surface of a computer-generated eye with a virtual scalpel. As the surgeon moves the handle, a robot arm moves the real scalpel blade over the real patient. (The "real" patient is actually a physical model of a human head.) The connection between the surgeon and the robot arm is modified by the computer interface, which eliminates slight tremors from the surgeon's hand and can scale down the surgeon's actions, for example, changing a 1-inch cut to a 1-millimeter cut.

Physical Therapy in a Virtual World

Unfortunately, many maladies cannot be cured either by surgery or by medication. Such a malady is Parkinson's disease, a brain function disorder that causes uncontrollable shaking and interferes with various motor skills. No one knows what causes Parkinson's disease, but it seems to be related to the death of brain cells that manufacture a neurotransmitter called dopamine. The disease also seems to be partly related to age—more than 60 percent of the people who get Parkinson's are over 50 years old. There is no cure for Parkinson's; the symptoms of the disease can be temporarily offset by certain prescription drugs, but these drugs eventually fail to have any effect.

The most serious effect of Parkinson's is *akinesia*, trouble walking or starting any type of sustained motion. Many people who suffer from Parkinson's either cannot get moving or move only in fits and starts. Strangely, though, many people with akinesia find that they can walk normally if certain kinds of visual cues are placed at their feet. Evenly spaced horizontal shapes, such as playing cards or lines, seem to trigger normal walking responses in the brain. This phenomenon is called *kinesia paradoxa*, a term that translates as "paradoxical walking."

Dr. Tom Riess, a California podiatrist who suffered from Parkinson's, knew about kinesia paradoxa, having developed a serious case of akinesia while in his mid-40s. He also knew about the burgeoning field of virtual reality. In particular, he was interested in a visor-based device called the Virtual Vision Sport. The device displayed video images on the inside of a clear plastic shield much like that on a set of one-piece sunglasses. Riess thought that this display could be used to trigger the walking response with virtual, rather than physical, cues.

Riess went to the company that made the eyewear with his idea to harness it as a therapeutic device. The company, Virtual Vision, referred him to the HIT Lab, in particular to researcher Suzanne Weghorst. Riess and Weghorst gathered a team of HIT Lab and Virtual Vision researchers and created a simple program that projected a series of lines advancing toward the viewer. When the system was tested on Riess and on another Parkin-

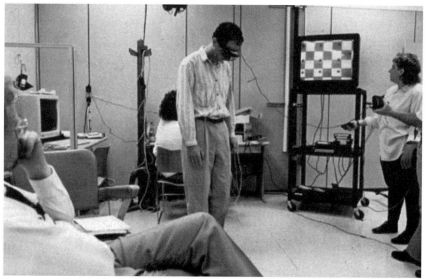

Dr. Tom Riess and researchers at the HIT Lab experiment with a therapeutic VR program designed to help Parkinson's disease patients handle problems with walking that are caused by the disease.   (Courtesy HIT Lab)

son's disease patient, both men started walking more easily. Riess found that he could walk with more confidence even after he took off the visor, though he had to concentrate on his walking more than someone without Parkinson's would. The results were so promising that Riess founded a company, HMD Therapeutics, to improve the system that projected the lines and make it available to others who suffer from Parkinson's disease.

VR therapy can also be used to help people handle even more serious disabilities. At the Oregon Research Institute in Eugene, Oregon, Dr. Dean Inman has developed a virtual environment that can help people learn how to use wheelchairs. Inman's program is similar to the project that shows how to adapt building plans for those who are wheelchair-bound. However, while the architectural simulator passively monitors how many times the wheelchair wheels turn, the Oregon Research Institute project actively controls how the wheelchair acts in the virtual environment. The wheelchair sits on a platform rigged to give feedback through the wheels of the chair. Steering the chair through the simulation with a joystick, the user can sense how it feels to ride over smooth sidewalks, rough dirt paths, and patches of ice. The simulator also lets the user steer through different rooms that range from spacious to cluttered, and even provides training in off-road navigation with a virtual grass-covered hill.

Fighting Phobias in a Safe Environment

Phobias are extreme fears of things (such as spiders) or situations (such as riding in elevators). The word *phobia* itself is a Greek word that means "fear." Some people develop phobias as the result of traumatic events. Falling off a tall jungle gym on a playground, for instance, can cause a child to develop a lifelong fear of heights, or *acrophobia*. Other people develop phobias for no apparent reason; such phobias can include the fear of flying or even the fear of being outdoors.

Some people fight their phobias with months or years of psychological analysis, medication or relaxation techniques to reduce anxiety, and gradual immersion therapy that slowly exposes a person to the object of his or her fear. Other people can take a more drastic approach, such as overcoming acrophobia by jumping off a high diving board into a swimming pool. A number of researchers have been using virtual reality to provide a comfortable middle ground between these two extremes.

Acrophobia lends itself very easily to virtual reality simulations. Using virtual architecture techniques, therapists can create environments that reproduce, and even exaggerate, the visual cues that trigger acrophobia. A California researcher, Dr. Ralph Lemson of the Kaiser-Permanente Medical Group's Department of Psychiatry, developed one particularly terrifying scenario. His environment showed a café patio, complete with a black-and-white tile floor and umbrella-shaded tables, hanging in midair over San Francisco Bay, with a plank leading to a representation of the Golden Gate Bridge. Volunteers who suffered from acrophobia donned HMDs and were asked to step onto the patio, walk over the plank, and stroll around on the bridge.

Dr. Lemson and his assistants monitored the volunteers' heart rate and blood pressure while the tests were going on, as well as talking to the volunteers and asking how they felt. The simulation caused the same reactions in the volunteers—shortness of breath, vertigo, and anxiety—that they felt in the real world. However, the ability to step away from the virtual environment helped the volunteers to withstand the simulation for gradually longer periods. Once they were comfortable with the virtual environment, the volunteers went on to meet real-world challenges that included driving across a bridge and riding up a building inside a glass elevator.

The success of this type of virtual therapy can be seen by the results of the first series of tests Dr. Lemson conducted. Thirty-two of Dr. Lemson's patients participated in the virtual

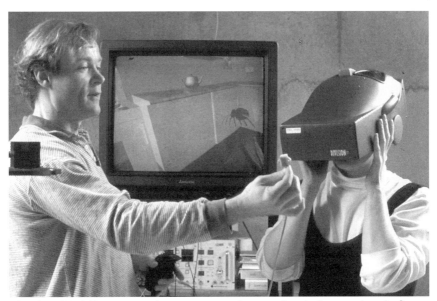

"Spider World" is a virtual environment designed to help people who are scared of spiders fight their fear. A computer-generated kitchen, complete with two virtual spiders and a 3-D spider web, is the central aspect of this VR therapy. Therapists also use a furry toy spider to give phobics the sensation of touching virtual spiders. This "mixed reality" technique adds to the realism of the VR display.   (Courtesy HIT Lab)

environment; all but two or three were able to overcome their fear of heights in the real world. Similar results have been reported by other researchers studying the use of VR as a phobia fighter. At the University of Washington's HIT Lab, a virtual environment called Spider World has successfully helped some subjects conquer their extreme fear of spiders by exposing them to spiders in a virtual kitchen. And a number of researchers at Georgia Institute of Technology and Emory University in Atlanta have developed a virtual passenger airplane program that has drastically reduced the fear of flying in many test subjects.

8
$$\frac{}{V}$$

VR IN THE
BUSINESS WORLD

*T*he business world—including finance, retail sales, manufacturing, and even real estate—stands to reap great financial rewards from applying the tools of VR to its work. As in other fields, presenting data in easily understood three-dimensional forms promises to help people in these fields do their work more quickly. It also promises to give businesses more control over their work, both in the virtual world and in the real world.

Virtually Sound Investments

Some financiers are already using virtual reality systems that track the value of *securities* (stocks and bonds) or *commodities* (such as wheat, gold, or oil) in the world's financial markets. Investing in these markets is a complicated process. Take the stock market, for example. A *stock* is a share of ownership in a company. Many companies sell these shares of ownership to get money for projects that the companies cannot pay for any other way. Such a project might involve developing a new product line or building new factories. The new owners of the company, the *stockholders*, get a share of the company's yearly profits. This payment is called a *dividend*.

People who invest in the stock market make money a number of ways. They buy stock in a company that will make enough money to pay them a good-sized dividend every year. By holding on to their stock for a few years, these investors can eventually earn more money than they paid for their stock. Investors also buy stock in popular or particularly profitable companies, hold it for a short while until it value rises, and then sell it. Even though these investors might not collect any dividend money, the money they get from selling the stock can be equal to or greater than the dividends they would receive over a few years.

One of the more risky ways people "play the market" is to *sell short*, selling shares of stock they do not own. The seller borrows the stock from a stockbroker, a professional stock trader who buys and sells stock for other people. The seller and the broker both agree that the seller will replace the stock in a few days or weeks. When that day comes, the seller buys back enough shares to replace the borrowed shares and gives them to the broker. This method is a real gamble for the seller. If the stock's value drops, the seller can replace the borrowed shares for less than they sold for, earning a tidy profit. If the value rises, though, the seller can lose a lot of money. The stock only has to fall a few dollars to earn the seller a fortune or rise a few dollars to wipe the seller out.

Though selling short is extremely risky, none of the other means of stock investment are truly safe, either. A stock's value can plummet if people suddenly lose confidence in a company's ability to make money. On the other hand, many stockholders have sold their shares for a good price, only to see a company's fortunes, and its stock's value, suddenly skyrocket. Similar problems affect investments in *bonds* (loans made to a company or a government) and commodities.

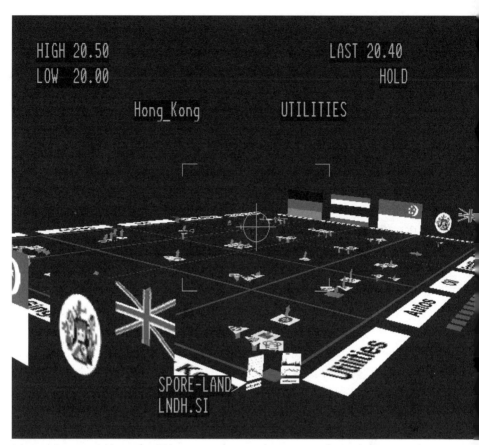

HIGH 20.50   LAST 20.40
LOW 20.00   HOLD

Hong_Kong   UTILITIES

SPORE-LAND
LNDH.SI

Maxus Systems' Metaphor Mixer can be used to create three-dimensional graphic representations of financial markets. In this image, the Metaphor Mixer displays promising stock offerings in Hong Kong and three other regions.   (Courtesy Maxus Systems International)

Tracking the value of stocks, bonds, and commodities is both a science and an art. Many professional investors make their living by buying and selling these investments for other people and taking a share of any profits their clients make. However, these *brokers* face a nearly overwhelming task every day. They must be able to track the minute-by-minute changes in the value of the various stocks, bonds, and commodities. They must know or be able to find out the latest news about any investment on the market. Finally, they must have at least some idea of how these investments will perform in the future.

Normally, brokers have to interpret data from thousands of stock, bond, and commodities trades. These data appear as lists of numbers displayed on computer screens or arranged on spreadsheets. These lists can include the history of a company's profits and losses, the value of a series of stock trades over a week, or even the number of barrels of oil shipped from various countries. Virtual reality can help speed the interpretation of this nearly endless flow of financial information. Indeed, a few companies have developed VR applications that transform market data into navigable virtual environments.

Two such applications are the Metaphor Mixer, developed by Maxus Systems International of New York, and Quantal PM (portfolio management), developed by Quantal International Inc. of California. Both of these applications use similar three-dimensional layouts to organize many types of financial data. They organize information into 3-D graphs, enhancing them with color, actions, and other special effects. Such an arrangement of data can easily draw an investor's eye to details that might be hidden in lists of gray numbers.

So far, some brokers and portfolio managers have been using these applications to monitor daily or weekly shifts in the value of their or their clients' holdings. One of the main concerns of investing is to achieve a balanced range of investments and not to have too much money tied up in a single area. Applications such as the Metaphor Mixer or Quantal PM let investors see at a glance where they are overextended, with too much of their money tied up in one area, or underextended, with too little money being placed in potentially lucrative markets.

One particularly difficult investment to forecast is the buying and selling of *futures*. Futures are contracts for the future delivery of such commodities as livestock, grain, metals, and other goods. For example, an investor who buys wheat futures is actually buying some or all of a farmer's crop while it is still in the fields. By paying for a crop months before harvest, the investor is gambling on the chance that he or she can sell it for more money when the crop comes to market.

Investors base the value of futures on how much these commodities might be worth when they finally come to market. Let's say that a commodities broker wants to monitor the future values of five items: oil, wheat, oranges, steel, and beef cattle. Using a VR system such as the Metaphor Mixer or Quantal PM, the broker would set up a three-dimensional graph to plot the values of various commodities.

To keep things simple, let's say that the broker wants to examine deliveries scheduled for next June, July, August, Sep-

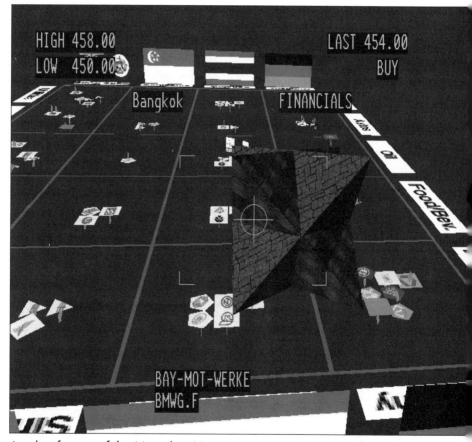

Another feature of the Metaphor Mixer is a computer-generated "agent" that draws the user's attention to a particularly noteworthy investment. Here, an agent (the geometric shape in the foreground) is trying to indicate that something interesting is happening in the financial market of Bangkok, Thailand. (Courtesy Maxus Systems International)

tember, and October. The base of the broker's virtual environment, then, would be a square graph made up of five units on a side, representing the five commodities and the five delivery months. Each combination of a commodity and a delivery month would have its own square on the graph. A column rising from the graph could represent the value of a particular future; the column's height could represent the value of the future or the rate at which the value is growing. If many people were buying and selling a particular future, its column could be colored a fiery red, while a future that few people were buying could be colored a cold blue.

Changing Store Layouts via VR

Just as virtual reality can help investors make money through better management of securities and commodities, it can help retailers make money through better sales practices. Grocery manufacturers—companies that make foodstuffs and household supplies—wage constant battles with each other to get people to buy their goods. They introduce new products, put old products into new containers, and try to convince store owners to put their products in areas where more people will see them.

It takes a great deal of time and effort to successfully package and position goods. So far, the only reliable way to estimate whether a product will sell well has been to conduct a series of surveys. Grocery manufacturers ask groups of shoppers whether they would buy a new product, even if it meant switching from one they already liked. Manufacturers also *test-market* new products, making small batches and selling them in a few cities around the nation. To determine whether changing product displays would help sales, manufacturers build mockups of store shelves and invite shoppers to select items as if they were shopping for real.

These methods all take a lot of money to set up and a long time to implement, and even then they do not always yield accurate results. For example, in the early 1990s a series of surveys suggested that many people would be willing to buy "clear" colas. Several soda companies began selling clear colas nationwide, only to cease production when it turned out that almost nobody bought them.

Virtual reality simulations of supermarket environments offer a less expensive and more efficient alternative to these other survey methods. Manufacturers have begun studying ways to use three-dimensional simulated supermarkets in place of full-scale mockups. Many of these environments are being tested using two-dimensional computer monitors, which still have better-quality images than do head-mounted displays. But these displays are still giving the manufacturers good data about how people shop. For instance, one of the United States' top frozen-foods companies wanted to find out what type of shelf arrangement was best for selling its product. Was it better to have foods grouped by item, or were shoppers more interested in finding a favorite brand? The company set up a virtual mockup of a supermarket's frozen-foods section, complete with representations of most of the major brands. Most supermarkets divide their freezer sections from left to right according to item, and top to bottom according to brand. The company set up the items in its virtual store using both this pattern and other arrangements. The company researchers used displays that grouped products according to brand names, package sizes, and even the prices most supermarkets charged. Trying to persuade the owner or manager of a real supermarket to make similar changes would have been impossible. By using a computer-generated environment, though, the company was able to tell which displays worked best for which types of frozen foods.

This does not mean that manufacturers are the only ones using VR. Store owners themselves are beginning to benefit from virtual reality. In 1995, the J. Sainsbury supermarket chain in Great Britain created a VR model of one of its stores that managers could travel through while wearing an HMD. The managers found that they could easily see the store from a shopper's perspective. They experimented with different aisle and shelf configurations to find arrangements that were more convenient. At the same time, they moved virtual models of various products around the shelves, seeking a pattern that gave better product placement. The chain found that using VR techniques, rather than building physical models or repeatedly altering the layouts of their real-world stores, saved a great deal of time and money.

Meeting Clients Virtually Anywhere

Meetings are an inescapable part of the business world. At least once a week in most companies, and in many cases one or two times a day, employees gather to discuss their work. Department heads talk about how well the company is doing as a whole and give each other updates on their departments' projects. Salespeople discuss ways to improve sales and how well they are selling various products. And workers go over anything that affects the work they do, from changes in assembly line procedures to ways to avoid on-the-job injuries. Meetings are the means by which companies organize their day-to-day operations.

In many cases, though, face-to-face meetings can be inefficient ways to exchange information. Construction projects require many meetings between architects, building contractors, city officials, and the projects' clients. Corporations that jointly develop new products have to hold meetings frequently to make sure that all parties are working toward the same goal. When all the people involved in the project live in the same or nearby cities, they can attend these meetings with little trouble. When the people live in cities that are far apart—across a state, in separate states, or in separate countries—traveling to meetings becomes a major hassle.

In the past few decades, teleconferencing has come about as an alternative to this long-distance commuting. People who gather in different cities speak to each other over the telephone or use closed-circuit television to send their images to each other. These long-distance conferences are useful if all the participants have the correct reports or displays in front of them and are meeting simply to discuss plans. Things become difficult, though, if one group does not have the latest copy of a report or if a phone connection goes bad. Also, teleconferences cannot offer the level of interaction found in a face-to-face meeting. A woman sitting in a conference room in Los Angeles, for example, cannot reach out and correct a figure on a wall chart in an office in New York.

During a conference in a virtual environment, this type of interaction *would* be possible. Using a set of reality simulators connected by a phone line, people could meet in a computer-generated conference room and interact much as they would in the physical world. Or they could meet in a model of a building that is being designed, or in any other meeting place they desired. While they were talking with each other, they could look at *avatars*, computer images that would represent each person at the meeting. These avatars could be a video image of each person, or they could be computer-generated images of anything from smile faces to wooden blocks to giant lobsters.

The difference between VR conferencing and other forms of teleconferencing would be the type of interaction that could take place. In a VR conference, a woman in Los Angeles *could* reach out and alter a chart made by a man in New York. The New York man could then save a copy of the altered computer-generated chart and use it to change the physical chart on the wall of his office. Other types of interaction would also be possible, such as going on a group tour of a factory floorplan and changing where equipment will be placed.

Not only *could* people in different cities interact with each other through VR, they already *are*. Bechtel Corp., an international building design firm, recently used VR's architectural design abilities as part of an immersive teleconferencing system. Bechtel was in charge of drawing up the plans for Dubai International Airport, a new airport being built in Saudi Arabia. Five separate groups around the world were handling different aspects of the project. The architects who designed the airport worked in San Francisco, but the structural engineers who checked the stability of the planned airport buildings were in London. The draftsmen who made the actual blueprints had their offices in Delhi, India. Finally, the manager of the project and the construction company that would build the airport had their headquarters in separate cities in Saudi Arabia.

Normally, representatives from each group would have spent days traveling to each other's offices as they coordinated their work. Virtual teleconferencing helped eliminate much of this time-consuming travel. The various groups consulted with each other using supercomputers that contained virtual mock-ups of the airport. As members of each group navigated through

Another way businesses could use VR would be as a means of monitoring far-flung computer networks. The CA-Unicenter TNG, depicted here, was created by business software firm Computer Associates International for just that purpose. This demonstration image shows how various components of a computer network could be depicted and controlled in a computerized environment. (Courtesy Computer Associates International)

their own computer's environment, avatars appeared in the models of the other groups. This way, all the participants could examine and alter different sections of the airport with little or no confusion. High-speed phone lines that transferred huge amounts of information made this intercontinental interaction possible.

Shopping for a House with VR

The same VR tools that make it easier to design buildings may one day make it easier to buy homes. Shopping for a house can be a time-consuming chore. Buyers can spend hours driving to and walking through different houses without finding one that fits their needs and desires. This process can be frustrating; often, the only results of a day of house-hunting are tired feet and disappointment. The process can also be frustrating for real estate agents who spend a lot of time taking clients around to houses that turn out to be just not right.

Some realty companies are looking into ways to use virtual models of the homes they have for sale to cut down on this fruitless activity. One system being considered uses a sort of video camera to take pictures of a house from many angles. A series of such images would be loaded into a VR computer, which would then assemble the image into a three-dimensional walkthrough. A prospective buyer could take a tour through such a model, seeing how it looks at different times of the day and even changing the color of the walls. The buyer would not have to travel to the real house until he or she knew it might be the right one.

Virtual Offices in Virtual Reality?

Virtual offices are an area of business that may or may not be affected by virtual reality. Virtual offices already exist, but they are not yet a part of VR. A virtual office is simply a collection of electronic gear—notebook computers, portable printers, cellular phones, and so forth—that salespeople or other office workers take on business calls. Many office workers actually do most of their productive work away from their offices. Salespeople, for example, are usually traveling to their customers' offices, demonstrating products, and writing orders. They use their offices mainly to clean up these orders, research prices, and create formal order forms that then have to go back to their customers for approval.

Instead of taking written orders back to a physical workplace, many salespeople have started sending their orders via fax machine or computer transfer. This practice makes it easier to sell more products to more people. Without having to go back to the office, salespeople avoid hours of unproductive travel time. The virtual office concept also saves money for the businesses that employ it. Instead of providing a separate room or separate desks in one big room for each employee, companies can reserve a few desks in a few rooms for work that must be done in a physical office.

None of this involves working with virtual environments—not yet, anyway. When VIEW was developed, one of its proposed uses was as a virtual desktop a worker could use to surround him- or herself with images of reports, graphs, and other documents. The worker could then select a document to read or edit, keeping the others around for easy access. Having these documents in virtual, rather than physical, form would carry certain advantages. There would be no worry of losing a document, as a simple search program could pinpoint the location of any document in the computer's memory. It would also be easy to copy, combine, and transfer documents, without having to worry about broken copy machines or empty staplers.

Right now, the VR tools available do not provide the type of image quality and ease of use that office workers would require. With proper advances, though, VR could be adapted to various business tasks. Salespeople and others could carry VR representations of physical offices with them. These offices might contain filing cabinets, shelves of reference books, and even representations of personal mementos that would never be broken by an avalanche of paperwork—and would never need dusting.

9

V

LEARNING, TRAINING, AND PLAYING IN VR

Virtual reality has a promising future as a tool of learning and recreation: educators ranging from elementary school teachers to university professors have been adapting VR as an instructional aid; corporations have been developing virtual reality job skill and safety programs that can quickly train new employees; and VR video game makers have been creating a wide range of environments in which people can play after a day in school or at work. VR will reach many people in these three areas as its presence expands over the next few decades. Relatively few people in the world are scientists, architects, doctors, or engineers. But most people have to go to school, most people receive on-the-job training, and most people at some point need to relax.

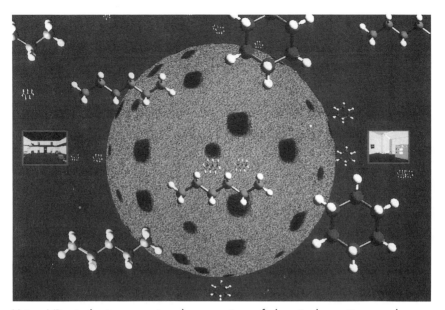

Using VR, students can get a close-up view of chemical reactions and other microscopic phenomena. (Image courtesy Dr. John Bell and Professor H. Scott Fogler of the University of Michigan Department of Chemical Engineering)

VR in the Classroom

Of the three areas, educational VR applications offer the most potential benefits for the least amount of money. Virtual reality is a fairly expensive technology. A high-quality system—with motion-tracked effectors, a sight-and-sound HMD, a control glove or other manipulation device, and a powerful reality simulator—can easily cost up to $10,000. Fortunately, virtual reality is also an extremely adaptable technology. It is possible to assemble a serviceable VR setup for less than $5,000 by connecting less expensive effectors to a good-quality personal computer.

At Kelly Walsh High School in Casper, Wyoming, computer programming teacher Becky Underwood is teaching 60 students a year how to create virtual environments on desktop computers. The students wear shutter glasses that turn images on the 2-D computer monitors into 3-D displays. They handle virtual objects with modified PowerGloves, control devices based on the

VPL DataGlove, that were manufactured by the Mattel toy company for Nintendo video games. To move around the environments, the students use computer mice or joysticks. And, at the end of each semester, they can examine their creations with a head-mounted display that cost about $400. Altogether, each of the school's 15 VR systems cost less than $2,500 to put together, with most of that money going to buy the computer that controls the system.

As simple as the systems are, Underwood's students have used them to create some remarkably sophisticated learning environments. One student, who was also studying Latin, used her computer to create a "Latin villa." Each room of the villa linked objects with Latin vocabulary words. As visitors left the villa, they were quizzed on the words they learned. Another student used his knowledge of calculus to create striking three-dimensional models of mathematical equations. One student even reproduced Fort Casper, the 19th-century U.S. Army fort that developed into the city of Casper, as a lesson in local history.

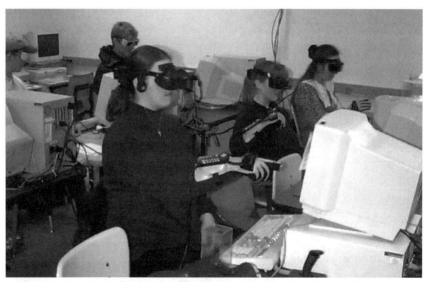

A growing number of schools offer classes in virtual reality, such as this one at Kelly Walsh High School in Casper, Wyoming. Kelly Walsh students have been designing and working with visual environments since 1994. (Courtesy of Becky Underwood, Kelly Walsh High School, Casper, Wyoming)

VR can be used to teach children how to use computers to create their own worlds and to tell stories about their creations. This image is from the NICE (Narrative, Immersive, Constructionist/Collaborative Environments) project developed for the CAVE.   (© 1996 Maria Roussos, Andy Johnson, Jason Leigh, Christina Vasilakis, Craig Barnes, and Thomas Moher, Electronic Visualization Laboratory and Interactive Computing Environments Laboratory, University of Illinois at Chicago)

Other schools in the United States and abroad have been doing similar work with the guidance of a number of universities. In Greenville, North Carolina, East Carolina University's Virtual Reality and Education Laboratory (VREL) has been giving advice on building and using VR systems to schools in North Carolina, West Virginia, California, and even New Zealand. One of VREL's codirectors, Dr. Veronica Pantelidis, has many suggestions of ways VR could enhance standard classroom activities. Civics classes could study local politics by creating virtual environment presentations on building-law changes; for example, creating a virtual model of a proposed factory near a housing tract, then analyzing how the factory would affect the lives of the people who lived there. Biology classes could study cell function by building 3-D models of real cells.

Younger students could also benefit from VR; in fact, some already have. In one case, at a school associated with VREL, a fifth-grade teacher used VR to help her students learn the shapes of basic geometric solids, such as pyramids, spheres, and cubes. The fifth graders were able to explore the interiors as well as the surfaces of these shapes, rapidly learning what each looked like and how they were put together. Later, when tested on such questions as what the base of a four-sided pyramid looked like, these students came up with the correct answer—a square— right away.

Other institutions have been addressing the educational uses of VR in other ways. The Virtual Reality Roving Vehicle (VRRV), a project of the HIT Lab in Seattle, took a van filled with VR equipment to a number of schools in the Pacific Northwest. The VRRV acted as a supplement to the subjects being studied in each school. In one typical application, the VRRV helped four classes at a junior high school study wetlands (such as swamps, marshes, ponds, and shallow lakes). Working together, the four classes built a VR model of a typical wetland. One class worked on the water cycle: how water enters a marsh or a pond and is used by the plants and animals within it. The other three classes worked on how wetlands collect and use energy, carbon (an element found in all living things), and nitrogen (another element that is especially important to plant life). When completed, the virtual wetland contained plant and animal life, including bacteria that fixed nitrogen in the soil. The students then donned HMDs, explored their virtual environment, and compared it to another model that had been created elsewhere.

Touring the Past with VR

The drive to make virtual reality available as a teaching aid is being carried on outside the academic world, as well. A number of companies have begun creating virtual environments that schools may one day use as part of their standard course of study. Some intriguing work is being done at Learning Sites Inc., which designs virtual learning environments based on ancient archaeological sites. The sites transported into VR range from Egyptian temples and Turkish religious communities to a beekeeper's farmhouse from ancient Greece. The Learning Sites staff takes all the information known about these sites, including the archaeologists' notes, and uses it to create three-dimensional models of the sites as they looked thousands of years ago.

In these interactive displays, students can examine how the buildings were put together and how they were decorated, and discover for themselves how each room was used. They can handle computerized representations of objects that archaeologists found when they were excavating the buildings. And they can read notes or listen to brief lectures on how archaeologists discovered the sites and uncovered their treasures. In an early project, a VR restoration of an ancient Egyptian fortress on the Nile River, visitors even had a virtual guide dressed as an Egyptian scribe who took them on a tour of the complex.

For the future, Learning Sites hopes to adapt its environments for multiple-user exploration. With appropriate advances in technology, one environment might host visitors from separate cities or different nations. Classes might one day tour VR archaeology sites with the assistance of the archaeologists who are running the excavation.

VR on Campus

Students in colleges and universities are also getting the opportunity to use virtual reality in their studies. At the University of Michigan at Ann Arbor, chemical engineering professors John T. Bell and H. Scott Fogler have developed a series of virtual environments that let students study the operation of chemical reactors and the design of chemical plants. Classroom lectures and textbook study can go only so far when dealing with such subjects. The only way students can truly understand how these systems work is to see them in action for themselves. Even better, students should be able to fiddle around with a chemical reactor's controls and see how their changes help or hinder reactions.

One set of environments that Bell and Fogler built, the VICHER modules (*VICHER* is short for *VI*rtual *CH*emical *R*eaction), give their students a safe way to gain this hands-on experience. Chemical plants are very hazardous operations, and the people in charge of them do not usually open them up to college tour groups. Those plants that do allow student tours restrict them to safe areas away from the main work areas, and naturally do not allow students any opportunities for hands-on work. The VICHER modules not only provide simulated versions of real-world equipment, but also let students watch simulated chemical reactions as they take place inside the simulated reactors. This type of observation, of course, would be impossible in the real world.

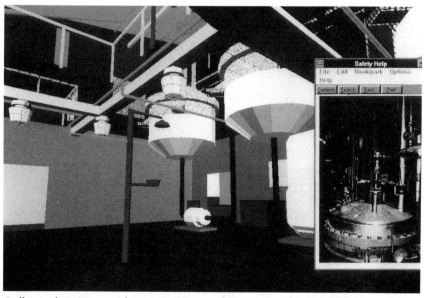

College chemistry students can tour and inspect a chemical plant using VICHER without exposing themselves to the physical dangers of visiting the actual facility.   (Image courtesy Dr. John Bell and Professor H. Scott Fogler of the University of Michigan Department of Chemical Engineering)

In papers Bell and Fogler have written on their work, however, they have pointed out that it will be a while before VICHER is truly ready to serve as a full-fledged education and research tool. As of January 1997, VICHER had been in development for about a year and was still in its early stages. It was also limited by the level of current VR technology. In spring 1996, 155 chemical plant design students participated in VICHER's first trial run. While most of them agreed that the simulator was impressive, most of them also agreed that the system itself needed work. They found that the head-mounted display's graphics were too small and blurry to be of much use. In an article on a different virtual environment—one that provided a tour of a chemical plant's hazards and safety systems—Bell and Fogler mentioned that all the students had to peek under the HMD at a regular computer monitor to read the signs posted in the virtual chemical plant. Still, the students also said that once VR technology improved, VICHER and the other VR applications would be very useful study and research tools.

High-Tech Training in Virtual Environments

VICHER, with its ability to safely expose college students to the hazardous environment of a chemical plant, also points to another educational use for virtual reality. Virtual environments can easily introduce new workers to unfamiliar or hazardous working conditions without the risk of on-site accidents. They can also be used to refresh and evaluate the skills of experienced employees by realistically reducing real-life working conditions.

Commercial flight simulators, which have been in use for decades, are an example of such training and evaluation applications. Airline pilots have benefited from computer simulations as much as fighter pilots. Just as work on military flight simulators led to much of the technology of virtual reality, virtual reality has done much to improve the quality of civilian flight simulators. With computer graphics, flight simulators can place pilots at or above almost any major airport in the world. To some purists, flight simulators are not really virtual reality systems. They do not give airline pilots a sense of being totally immersed within a virtual environment. Instead, pilots sit in a realistic mockup of an airplane cabin and view the computer-generated representation of an airport approach or a midair flight scene. The experience is made more realistic if the mockup is placed on a motion platform, a hydraulically controlled tilting table that can change the angle of the simulator. For all practical purposes, however, flight simulators as detailed as these are virtual reality: They use computers to generate and control realistic, three-dimensional environments that react to the actions of their participants.

In any case, flight simulators have inspired VR researchers and companies to create similar setups for other applications. One particularly popular area of research involves designing driving simulators that can be used for a host of safety studies and driver training programs. These driving simulators will re-create the sensations of driving through hilly countryside, along rough sections of roadway, or over rain-slick highways.

One of the most ambitious of these simulators is the Iowa Driving Simulator (IDS), which has been operating at the University of Iowa's Center for Computer-Aided Design since 1992. The IDS combines a mockup of an automobile's passenger compartment with a dome-shaped screen that fills the simulator driver's field of view. Like a flight simulator, the IDS is mounted on a motion platform that mimics the effects of acceleration and road vibration. Using the simulator, researchers study how drivers react to a range of driving conditions, determine whether changes in highway design would be beneficial, and run virtual prototyping tests of new vehicle designs and machinery. The simulator has even been used for medical research, through monitoring the effects of various medicines on drivers and evaluating the safety of a new type of prescription lens for glasses.

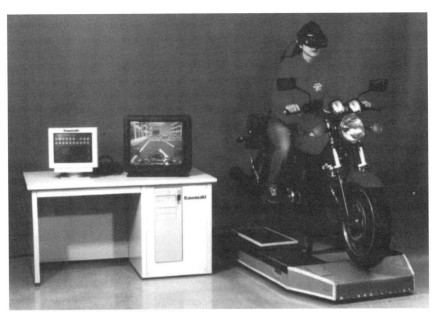

Kawasaki Heavy Industries and Virtuality KK combined forces in 1996 to create this simulator for student motorcycle riders. Using this system, students can make and learn from mistakes without risking their lives or the lives of others. Japan's traffic laws require that driving schools include simulation as part of their students' instruction. (Courtesy Virtuality Inc.)

Another highly advanced VR driving simulator, named "truck driVR," was developed in 1996 for Amoco, the Chicago-based American Oil Company. Every year, all of Amoco's truck drivers are tested by human evaluators who ride with them for a day. Amoco needed a reliable system that could replace this costly, time-consuming way of doing things. The oil company asked Bravo Multimedia, a firm that designs computerized training programs, to build the system. Bravo developed a system that combines a steering wheel and foot pedals designed for race car computer games, an HMD, and a highly detailed virtual environment complete with roads, highways, and other vehicles. The hardware alone cost less than $50,000—an amazing deal, considering that such a system would have cost more than $30,000 a year or two earlier. For its money, Amoco got a system that mimics the sensations of driving a tractor-trailer rig filled with 40,000 gallons of gasoline. Driving skills are tested by 21 typical driving hazards (including overly aggressive drivers, pedestrians crossing the street at the wrong time, and a deer jumping in front of the truck), all without risking the drivers, their cargo, or any bystanders.

VR-based driver safety training is not limited to four-wheeled vehicles. In Japan, the British VR firm Virtuality has teamed up with Kawasaki Motorcycle Co. to create a highly realistic motorcycle driving trainer. A student motorcycle rider mounts a real Kawasaki motorcycle that is mounted on a motion platform, then puts on a head-mounted display. As the student navigates the virtual driving environment, the motorcycle tilts, jitters, and otherwise responds to his or her movements. As with car and truck driving simulators, the Kawasaki simulator lets students make and learn from driving mistakes without risking their lives or the lives of other people.

Virtual Industrial Training

Factory workers may also benefit one day from VR simulations of hazardous environments. One of the most dangerous situations a factory worker faces is the factory floor itself during his or her first weeks on the job. New workers have to spend a lot of time gaining the experience needed to safely work with even a factory's least dangerous machines. New workers also have to spend a great deal of time getting used to how their factories are arranged. With immersive models of actual workspaces, companies could cut down the time it takes newly hired employees to learn how to do their jobs safely.

The Virtual Environments Laboratory at Northeastern University in Boston is exploring ways to simulate one dangerous factory job—using an overhead crane to move heavy objects. Accidents involving factory cranes kill nearly 10 workers and injure more than 1,600 others every year. Some of these deaths and injuries are caused by inexperienced or inattentive crane operators. Northeastern University researchers are using a fairly

By creating immersive mockups of factory floors, companies can both determine the base arrangement for equipment and safely expose new workers to their jobs.   (Courtesy Proslovia Clarus)

simple HMD-and-computer system to simulate factory crane operations in the hope that virtual environment training and evaluations will cut down these accidents. Their goal is to build a more detailed training environment in the near future.

VR and Entertainment

All work and no play can make VR a fairly dull technology. Fortunately, many researchers and companies have been hard at work making sure that VR has a fun side to balance its serious uses.

At the Electronic Visualization Lab (EVL) at the University of Illinois at Chicago, one of the most popular CAVE projects was "The Great Sandini Virtual Reality Circus of the CAVE." The project of an EVL graduate student, the circus featured many unusual VR exhibits contributed by the student's colleagues. Among these were a freak show (in which distorted

The MIT Media Lab's "Kids' Room" display is based on the lab's ALIVE projected VR system. Computer-generated characters, projected by cameras behind the large wall screens, respond to the girl's actions. (© 1996 Webb Chappell; Courtesy MIT Media Lab)

video images of the CAVE circus's visitors were the freaks) and a shooting gallery in which virtual marksmen shot snowballs at bouncing jack-in-the-boxes.

Researchers at the MIT Media Lab adapted their ALIVE projected VR system to their collegiate need for after-class excitement by creating SURVIVE, the Simulated Urban Recreational Violence Interactive Video Environment. The system is a merging of the Media Lab's ALIVE/Smart Room technology with the shoot-'em-up computer game DOOM, using a wired plastic rifle as the main effector. By running in place, players can navigate through the various levels of the game, ducking behind walls or snapping off a quick shot as they run for cover.

Of course, recreation is not just the domain of academic institutions. Many companies are capitalizing on virtual reality's ability to place people in exciting adventures as well as in educational environments. Virtuality, the company that created Kawasaki's motorcycle simulator, is also one of the world's biggest VR entertainment companies. Virtuality arcade games—which include starfighter assaults against the might of enemy alien strongholds and treasure hunts in sunken shipwrecks amid sharks and pirates' ghosts—are in amusement centers around the world. These games use head-mounted displays and control wands made by Virtuality to withstand the heavy use dished out by arcade game enthusiasts.

These VR experiences are so popular that other companies are eager to develop games for Virtuality systems. One such joint effort yielded the Winchester Total Recoil shooting simulator, which features a true-to-life replica of the Winchester Model 101 sport shotgun. The simulator gives an incredibly realistic recreation of what it feels like to fire a shotgun at clay discs or other targets. Real shotguns "kick" quite firmly when fired. To mimic this effect, the simulated shotgun is fitted with a small carbon dioxide thruster that shoots out a puff of gas each time the gun fires. The CO_2 blast is powerful enough to create the kick that shotgun shooters expect. The simulator is so real that shooting clubs and other sporting organizations buy it as a means to safely train new shooters.

Virtual Worlds within a Virtual World

Another major VR entertainment company has taken the concept of virtual environments a step beyond their application to computers. Virtual World Entertainment of Chicago operates a chain of virtual reality arcades around the world that are organized on a single theme: the supposed existence of the Virtual Geographic League, which was founded in 1895 by scientific pioneers who created a space-and-time machine that allowed them to travel to distant worlds. In the Virtual World game centers, visitors can climb into modern versions of these travel pods and transport themselves into one of two adventures. In

Just as fighter simulators immerse their pilots in mock-ups of airplane cockpits, some VR entertainment companies immerse game players in full-size extensions of virtual environments. Pictured here is the Tesla simulator pod developed by Virtual World Entertainment for its BattleTech and Red Planet adventure games. (Courtesy Virtual World Entertainment, Inc. © 1996)

one scenario, the players are in control of a huge BattleMech, a warrior robot that fights alongside and against other battle machines on a far-distant desert planet. In the other adventure, the players race hovercraft through man-made canals on Mars in the year 2054.

The cockpits used for both these gaming scenarios are very complex, featuring more than 100 controls that can be used or ignored according to each player's skill and interest. Speakers placed throughout the cockpit create three-dimensional sound effects, such as the throb of hovercraft engines or the tromp of a BattleMech's legs. Three-dimensional visual effects are created with an autostereoscopic flat-panel display screen. As mentioned in Chapter Four, an autostereoscopic display does not require users to wear any special equipment. Computer graphics are rendered in a way that tricks the eyes and brain into perceiving a 3-D environment by seeming to focus them behind the display screen.

To enhance the immersion within the virtual gaming environments, Virtual World's gaming centers are set up as Victorian-era adventurers' clubs, complete with mission briefing centers, oak-paneled meeting rooms, and plush lounges. A typical session takes up to half an hour: 10 minutes to teach players how to use the equipment, 10 minutes of game time, and a 10-minute debriefing period in which each game is evaluated. These centers have been popular enough for Virtual World to start offering national and world championships for each of its gaming scenarios.

VR Gaming at Home

The main drawback to these VR arcade games is their expense. Serious game players can easily spend from $10 to $100 at a time in their desire to become proficient in playing these games. A less expensive alternative would be to put together a VR gaming system at home, provided they could find equipment that was cheap enough.

Fortunately, inexpensive VR equipment has been around since 1989. The Mattel PowerGlove, mentioned earlier, was a VR glove controller that was manufactured for the Nintendo Entertainment System video game player. It was based on the VPL Research DataGlove, but used plastic strips covered with metallic ink, rather than optical fibers, to monitor how the fingers flexed. A game control panel on the back of the glove allowed users to fully interact with both regular games and games designed especially for the glove. A transducer on the back of the glove emitted ultrasonic pulses that were picked up by a receiver attached to the Nintendo unit, allowing the system to track the glove. The glove was a big seller for Mattel. It was popular not just with video gamers, but also with VR system builders, who saw it as a cheap alternative to the more expensive gloves that used fiber optics or other devices to measure finger positions. The PowerGlove was not as accurate as these other gloves, but at under $100 a pair it was a hard deal to beat.

Other virtual reality gaming gear came on the market as the 1990s progressed. Nintendo, seeing the popularity of the PowerGlove, developed a goggle-style stereoscopic display called the Virtual Boy. It was fairly unsophisticated compared to full-scale HMDs: It displayed games in just one color—red—and was attached to a tripod that rested on a tabletop. To use it, gamers had to position themselves so their faces were even with the goggles and then hold their heads steady during game play. Even so, it was the only low-priced VR display available for a year or two, and as such it earned an acceptable amount of money for its makers.

Recently, companies such as Virtual i-O and Virtual Vision, both of Seattle, have developed less restrictive visor-style HMDs that can be used with desktop computers. And shutter glasses can be purchased in many computer and electronics stores for less than $100 a pair. As these types of personal VR devices become more prevalent, more computer and home video games will be made to capitalize on their multidimensional abilities.

10
V

VIRTUAL REALITY IN THE MILITARY

When most people use VR to simulate hazardous environments or difficult tasks, they are looking for ways to minimize their risks. When members of the armed forces use VR to simulate hazardous environments or difficult tasks, they are simply preparing for a day at the office. For members of the armed forces, "the office" can be a block of sky that opposing air forces wish to control, a battlefield, or a stretch of harbor leading to the open ocean. All of these locales, and many others, are being simulated in virtual reality.

Things happen so quickly in combat that soldiers, sailors, and pilots can easily become overwhelmed. Armies, navies, and air forces train constantly to keep this from happening, preparing for the time their skills are called upon. Since the fall of the Soviet Union in the early 1990s, however, nations around the world have been shrinking their armed forces and spending less money on the troops who are left. Budget cuts mean that armed forces cannot do as much real-life training as they might need.

Modern flight simulators can project quite detailed images onto dome screens that surround the pilot. The little block on top of the pilot's helmet is a motion tracker that lets the simulator adjust the display based on which way he is looking. (Evans & Sutherland Computer Corp.)

Combat exercises risk the lives of the people who are involved, cost millions of dollars, and put an enormous amount of wear and tear on equipment. With less money available, many services around the world are developing ways to mimic military tasks in the relatively cheaper arena of VR.

Beyond SuperCockpit

VCASS, the Visually Coupled Airborne Systems Simulator developed by Thomas Furness (who later founded the University of Washington's HIT Lab), was just the first step toward the use of virtual environments in the military. SuperCockpit, the pro-

---

gram that would have improved VCASS as a high-tech tool for controlling warplanes, had to be abandoned in the late 1980s. The U.S. Air Force, which had commissioned the program, saw that virtual environment substitutes for or enhancements of physical flight controls were beyond the technology of the time. Even using HMDs for flight simulation was stretching the ability of most VR systems. These days, however, the technology promises to become a very nice substitute for the large, expensive flight simulators currently in use.

This is not to say that these simulators are inefficient. With the computer technology boom of the 1980s, the quality of military (and civilian) flight simulators skyrocketed. These days, pilots can train in full-scale cockpits placed inside minitheaters mounted on motion platforms. Dome-shaped screens surround the pilots with simulated scenes of airports and cloud-filled skies. As the pilot "flies" the simulator, the motion platform tilts and shakes to provide the sensations of flight. Other systems use

A simpler but more portable example of a modern flight simulator. The three-screen display, cockpit mockup, and controlling computer can be disassembled and sent to various air bases far more easily than can larger full-motion simulators.   (Evans & Sutherland Computer Corp.)

nonmoving cockpits with smaller, flat-screen displays that still give much of the feeling of air-to-air combat.

Improvements in computer graphics alone have contributed much to the quality of the simulation. Instead of grid-shaped landscapes and simplified icons of hostile targets, such as those in VCASS, modern simulators allow pilots to fly over realistic terrain and engage true-to-life enemy aircraft. Some simulators monitor which way their pilots look, using motion trackers attached to standard helmets, and adjust the display accordingly.

But the desire for an HMD-based simulator still exists, especially since HMDs are no longer the bulky, million-dollar bug-eyed helmets of VCASS. Portable, less expensive VR trainers would be a cost-effective alternative to the larger simulators. Such a trainer is being considered to accompany the new Joint Strike Fighter, a warplane being designed to replace older aircraft in the 21st century. And there is already talk of mounting some of the fighter's displays on the pilot's helmet—a possible step back toward the idea of the SuperCockpit.

A Wide DIStribution of Military VR

Fixed-wing aircraft are not the only military vehicles that are being simulated in VR. In the United States alone, a host of virtual war machines, from the AH-64A Apache helicopter to the M1A1 Abrams tank, have computerized counterparts that combine physical mockups with immersive computer displays. As an added benefit, simulators in separate cities, separate states, and even separate countries will eventually be linked for large-scale simulated combat missions. A system called Distributed Interactive Simulation (DIS) is being developed to link many different types of simulators to a shared virtual battlefield. Such a widely distributed system would help the various services avoid a serious problem that crops up during wartime: the difficulty in synchronizing the actions of the thousands of troops, vehicles, and weapons during wartime.

No major battle is ever unplanned. Aside from chance meetings between small fighting units, in every engagement both sides start out following carefully drawn plans. Each service receives orders describing where troops will move, where artillery and aircraft will bombard enemy positions, or where warships will launch rockets, land troops, or engage enemy shipping. These plans rarely last beyond the first few minutes of a battle, but they are always available at the start.

Part of the reason why battle plans almost never last is that the thousands of soldiers, vehicles, and weapons involved have usually never worked together on a grand scale. Invariably, things will go wrong. A tank group will move out at the wrong time or will lose track of where it is; a communications relay will break down; a squadron of ground-attack planes will be prevented from supporting allied troops by heavy anti-aircraft fire. The commanding officers of all the forces involved have to work around such problems in a matter of minutes, if not seconds, to keep the tide of battle from turning against them. Such rapid adjustments can cause further problems, or they can succeed, depending on how well the forces involved work together. DIS training, by combining simulators from various branches of the military, can help build these needed techniques of teamwork.

Individual Tactics in a Virtual Combat Zone

Individual soldiers may also learn to handle the stresses of combat in virtual environments. Unlike war movies, real combat is not choreographed. Every instant spent advancing through a combat zone or patrolling unfamiliar territory exposes soldiers to a spectrum of real and possible dangers. Enemy snipers can suddenly open fire from inside a building. Booby-trapped explosives can wipe out whole squads in an instant. Even normally harmless things, such as fog, can hide potential dangers from an advancing unit. Training mentally prepares men and women to handle these dangers as much as it exposes them to the techniques of fighting. Researchers at such institutions as the Naval Postgraduate School in Monterey, California, and STRI-COM—the U.S. Army's Simulation, Training, and Instrumentation Command—in Orlando, Florida, have been designing VR systems that can help give soldiers the edge in battle.

The Dismounted Infantry Virtual Environment (DIVE) program is one such system. It combines virtual environments developed for use with DIS simulators with single-person VR effectors, including special wired replicas of the weapons nor-

U.S. Army Capt. Russel Storms experiments with the Omni-Directional Treadmill created by Dr. Mike Zyda at the Naval Postgraduate School in Monterey, California. This device is one of many being developed that would allow troops to navigate virtual combat experiences almost as easily as they move around in the real world.   (Courtesy Dr. Mike Zyda, Naval Postgraduate School)

mally carried into combat. It also uses highly realistic computer-generated soldiers as participants in the simulated missions. With such a system, a trainee squad leader (an experienced soldier who is in charge of a group of up to 10 others) can issue orders to a squad of virtual troops as if they were in a real firefight. Such virtual missions might include clearing out a building full of enemy troops that are also created by the computer.

Moving around these virtual environments is perhaps the biggest problem that needs to be solved. The cords that connect HMDs and other effectors to their reality simulators severely limit how far soldiers can walk in physical space. Researchers are working around this limitation by testing a number of innovative devices that allow unlimited movement in virtual space. One such device looks like a computerized unicycle that pivots in a complete circle. By pedaling and tilting their bodies, soldiers can walk in any direction in a virtual environment. They can even fire back at their virtual foes: The system monitors which way the soldiers' weapons point with mechanical sensors mounted on the soldiers' arms.

Another device developed by a group of researchers at the Naval Postgraduate School offers a more natural way to walk in VR. The Omni-Directional Treadmill has two separate moving belts that cross at a 90-degree angle, looping over motorized rollers that make the belts easier to walk on. Treadmills offer the most natural way to move in virtual environments, but have always suffered from two drawbacks. They require some other device for users to change direction, such as a set of pivoting handlebars. And no matter where the user steers in the virtual environment, the treadmill itself gives only the feeling of walking in a straight line.

The Omni Directional Treadmill allows soldiers to walk in any direction, just as the two wired rollers in a mouse allow computer users to move a pointer anywhere on the monitor's screen. To keep from rolling off the edge, users wear a belt and a harness that keeps them centered on the treadmill's surface.

Another method of moving through a military VR simulation involves the SARCOS® IPORT®, a stationary unicycle that allows participants to pedal their way through virtual environments. (Courtesy Naval Postgraduate School and SARCOS®)

Only one of these treadmills existed as of early 1997, but it was so widely praised by those who used it that improved versions are being developed.

To the Sea in Simulated Ships

Military simulators can be used to simulate a host of noncombat environments as well. The U.S. Navy is currently working on VR training programs for two vital aspects of life on board military vessels. One program, being developed by the Naval Research Laboratory's Advanced Technology Branch, teaches new submarine officers how to navigate surfaced subs through a harbor. Surface navigation is a very tricky operation: Submarines weigh thousands of tons and cost millions of dollars, and the officer in charge of safely steering through a harbor could effectively end his career by running the sub aground or hitting another vessel. Yet a young officer has very little time to learn to be an officer of the deck (the official term for this position). Submarines spend most of the time submerged and very little time sailing through harbors. A VR training system would speed the time it takes to master this tricky task.

Another vital noncombat task that requires a lot of training is fighting fires on board ship. A fire is one of the most serious disasters that can befall a ship. Many sailors prefer the idea of having a hole punched into the hull of their ship over having a fire break out. A hole can be patched fairly quickly; sailors are trained to use mattresses, lockers, spare wood, and anything else that is handy as temporary plugs. Naval vessels are equipped with watertight doors that can isolate any flooding to a few compartments, even if the hole cannot be patched.

But a fire on board a ship can quickly get out of hand; almost every space in a ship contains fuel, oil, ammunition, paint, or other flammables. When these materials burn, they give off thick smoke and poisonous gases that can rapidly fill the compartments inside the ship's hull. Even with the firefighting gear carried aboard every ship, sailors can find themselves on the losing side of a battle with a fire if they are not careful. The Naval Research Laboratory is working on a VR system to give sailors a greater edge over fires. Its system is based on a virtual replica of the ex-USS *Shadwell*, an old troop landing ship that the Navy uses to conduct experiments with new firefighting techniques and equipment. The computerized environment can replicate the many types of fires that have broken out in Navy ships over the years.

The virtual *Shadwell* proved its potential worth as a training tool in exercises that paired it with the real training vessel. Two teams of experienced Navy firefighters were given the task of navigating through the real ship as if they were putting out a fire. To make the task realistic, the face plates of the firefighters' masks were partially obscured to give the effect of looking through billowing clouds of smoke. The firefighters who explored the virtual environment before going through the physical exercise did better than those who only studied the ship's blueprints. In one case, the crew that went through the VR simulations performed the physical drill roughly half a minute faster. Half a minute may not sound like such a great achievement, but in the real world, half a minute can mean the difference between saving and losing a ship and its crew.

DOOMed to Oppose the Marines

The highly advanced simulators presently being developed may one day find widespread use throughout the armed forces. But many of these technological marvels share one drawback: They cannot be easily taken apart and shipped out when a military unit is sent overseas. Yet simple levels of simulation are pointing the way to portable VR trainers. In 1995, the U.S. Marine Corps began adapting the three-dimensional shoot-'em-up game DOOM as an urban combat trainer for its four-member fire teams. An add-in package transforms DOOM's Martian landscapes into a computerized replica of a real Marine Corps training site, and the game's hell-spawned monsters into well-armed human foes (modeled on posable toy soldiers).

Though not as detailed as fully immersive VR systems—the Marines' fire team trainer runs on up to four regular desktop PCs—the modified DOOM game has a good number of benefits of its own. Because it is used on computers that are inexpensive and easy to transport, the trainer can be used almost anywhere the Marines go. A typical Marine serves a three-year tour, spending most of that time on board a navy ship, according to 1st Lt. Scott Gordon, who was exposed to the game in the Marine Corps' Systems Command. "If, for example, we have to clear an [American] embassy, then ideally we could have a bitmap of every embassy in the world that the Marines protect, and that could be each scenario," Gordon explains. Training for such a mission would be as simple as loading the proper map into the computer and booting up the game.

Though "Marine DOOM" is restricted to standard 2-D computer screens, further versions of the game may one day be adapted to the tools of VR. But "Marine DOOM" showed it was realistic enough to teach fire teams how to work together. "The benefit of it is working on the mental aspect of combat," says Gordon. And truly, the best that any simulation system can do is mentally prepare its users for the challenges of the real world. "Computer simulation will never replace field training, but field training will never replace war," Gordon points out. "You know, in basketball, the only way to learn how to do free-throws well in a game is to do lots of free-throws."

11
∇

REAL DRAWBACKS
TO VIRTUAL REALITY

*V*irtual reality has generated great interest and enthusiasm since news of its development broke in the late 1980s. A new technology such as virtual reality can be exciting, especially since it offers people a tool to enhance their lives. Virtual reality gives people opportunities to work in artificial worlds in ways that cannot be duplicated in the physical world—an awesome technological benefit. But no new technology is without problems, not even VR. For all its interesting and innovative applications, VR has a number of physical, technological, and ethical drawbacks. To understand how VR can realistically fit into the modern world, we need to examine its problems as well as its potential.

Cyberhype: Mistaking Pipe Dreams for Predictions

Unfortunately, when an innovative new technology such as virtual reality comes about, people often cannot distinguish between what it *might* be able to do and what it truly *can* do. Aside from systems used in entertainment, most VR systems are still in the experimental stage. Even those being used by industrial designers are little more than highly advanced versions of

Virtual reality allows amazingly realistic reproductions of exhilarating experiences. But these experiences are usually created especially for highly advanced VR systems, and are considered to be exceptional demonstrations rather than run-of-the-mill applications.   (Evans & Sutherland Computer Corp.)

working prototypes. Virtual reality is at the same stage of development in the late 1990s as the automobile was in the early 1900s: It works; people can use it to do many things they could not do otherwise; but it still does not have the capabilities it will have in the future.

Throughout these early years, however, virtual reality has been presented to the world as being more advanced and more easy to use than it really is. In newspaper articles, magazine features, and TV reports about VR, much attention has been given to the great technological advance VR represents. It is true that VR is a significant achievement. Never before, without resorting to full-scale models, has anything even come close to replicating the sensations of the physical world. But these media reports have paid far less attention to the problems VR researchers are trying to solve—problems such as low picture resolution in HMDs and long lag times between a user's actions and their effect upon the virtual environment.

As a result, many people who are not directly involved in the field hold views of VR that are falsely optimistic. In fact, people could even get the impression that VR is a miraculous gadget that lets its users handle and alter information as easily as handling and cooking food in a kitchen. True, people may be able to explore distant lands and experience other cultures using VR without leaving their homes. And they may be able to change aspects of their lives, from their personalities to their wardrobes, by first testing out these changes in artificial worlds. But they cannot do so now.

While dreams of what the technology might bring about are attractive, and many applications of VR come close to fulfilling these dreams, such dreams are far in advance of anything current VR could realistically accomplish. Yet because the dreams *are* so very appealing, media coverage has emphasized them, often excluding VR's real capabilities. Thus, the exaggerated promotion of the technology's benefits has created an aura of media hype surrounding virtual reality. And those who are attracted by the hype of VR soon find themselves facing the reality of its limitations.

As mentioned in Chapter Five, HIT Lab researcher Dace Campbell is heavily involved in developing VR as a tool for architecture. When he started working with VR in 1993, he found that the real technology did not quite live up to the accounts of how it was poised to change the future of computing. "I came to the lab and found that the technology isn't anywhere near where I thought it was," he says. "And so I spent a lot of my time writing and trying to organize more the ways [people and VR systems] can interact than actually making them interact."

Campbell has found that this trend has not stopped: "One of the frustrating things for me as a researcher is that the media often portrays technology as being 'here,' 'now,' 'today.' And that's dangerous, because people get 'there' and it whets their appetites a little bit, and then they understand just how far away it is and they walk away disappointed and frustrated. So its very easy, I think, for the media to capture an idea that *will* come and say that it's already here."

Fortunately, he adds, reality is quickly catching up to the fantasy: "The flip side of the argument is that it's just about here. We're actually finding, as researchers, that we're very ready to go out into the real world now."

Despite the inconvenience of reading between the lines of media hype, the hype itself is merely something that stemmed from overenthusiasm, not something created by the technology itself. But the tools used to mimic the physical world *do* have drawbacks of their own.

The Physical Drawbacks of Virtual Reality

Even though virtual reality is a computing technology, it involves strapping equipment onto the human body. All but one or two types of virtual reality systems require their users to wear some sort of apparatus. The most commonly used piece of VR body-wear is, of course, the head-mounted display. Compared to the Sword of Damocles, which had to be supported by a metal post, modern HMDs are very light. Some full-sized HMDs weigh as little as 4.5 pounds, while visor displays such as shutter glasses weigh even less.

Unfortunately, this weight is placed on top of the head and spinal column, a structure that can be thought of as a bowling ball on top of a pipe cleaner. HMD manufacturers do their best to ensure that the weight of their displays is evenly balanced. Even so, the muscles and the vertebrae of the neck must adjust themselves to support and control this extra weight. And shutter glasses require their users to hold their heads fairly straight and steady as they work with their virtual environments. Not only do users have to maintain the 3-D illusion, but they cannot move their heads so far that the interface cords yank off the glasses. The added strain on the head and neck muscles can cause headaches and muscle aches, especially after long VR sessions.

Cyberspace Sickness

When we move, our bodies register more sensations than just the change of view. Our muscles signal the brain that they are moving and tell it in which direction they are doing most of their work. Skin cells sense the slight breeze created as we swing our arms and legs around, and the changes of temperature as we move into and out of sunlight. We even carry our own position trackers on each side of our head: Each inner ear contains three fluid-filled tubes called the semicircular canals, which make horizontal and vertical loops. As we shake or nod our heads, the fluid shifts around, triggering nerve cells that send signals about the position changes to the brain. This and other information from the inner ears helps us keep our balance.

In some people, this process malfunctions. The inner ears can send movement signals when a person is not moving or fail to send the proper signals when that person *is* moving. Such misfirings cause vertigo: sensations of extreme dizziness, nausea, and confusion that make people think they are falling when they are on solid ground. Motion sickness—car sickness, sea sickness, air sickness—can also be caused when the body's motion sensors fail to catch up with rapid changes in position.

A similar but opposite problem occurs for some people when they work with virtual reality. In VR, users' bodies generally stay in one place, even though users see their perspectives change as they move through a virtual environment. VR users move their heads and arms as they interact with the environment, but they do not experience the proprioceptive cues that would accompany moving their bodies across space. *Proprioception* is the body's own sense of movement that comes from special nerve cells called, appropriately, proprioceptors—in the muscles, bones, joints, and skin. The discrepancy between what a VR user sees and what he or she feels can create symptoms similar to those of motion sickness. Called *cyberspace sickness* or simply *cybersickness*, the feelings of nausea and disorientation limit how long some people can work with HMD-based VR systems.

Decompressing from VR

Yet another problem VR users have to contend with is the disorientation they go through after working in virtual environments for a long time. People who work with regular, nonimmersive desktop computers have similar problems. Users see reality as somewhat "unreal" after focusing on a computer's monitor screen for hours on end. This sensation can last from a couple of minutes to more than half an hour, depending on the individual and how long he or she has been working.

People perceive computer graphics environments and the physical world differently. In the images we see of the physical world, shadows blend smoothly with the edges of objects, small items can easily be separated from each other, and objects at medium-to-long distances can be noticed, if not identified. Computer graphics, on the other hand, are made up of sharp edges and lines. Even when created by advanced graphics supercomputers, objects that seem smooth and round are made up of angled polygons and combinations of differently shaded color blocks called *pixels*. Computer graphics artists use a range of programming techniques to smooth out the rough edges and create the illusion of curved surfaces. Even so, the eyes and brain have to work harder to perceive and translate the computer images as something approaching the physical world.

The type of display a system uses also makes a difference. Even though it is barely noticeable, cathode-ray tubes constantly flicker as their electron beams scan over the face of a display screen. People do not usually notice this flickering, but its presence does strain the user's eyes. Liquid-crystal displays do not have the flicker problem of CRTs, but they do not have the tight picture definition of a typical CRT, either. Instead, LCD screens form images by combining hundreds or thousands of pixels into patterns that the brain blurs into a coherent image. In HMDs that use liquid-crystal displays, the screens are so close that users tend to focus on the individual blocks of color, not the images they create. Users often have to squint to blur the pixels into a recognizable image; this causes headaches.

Then there are the psychological problems that crop up when people spend a long time working in VR. Because the immersive VR experience comes mostly from visual and audio simulation, only the visual and audio processing areas of the brain receive any real stimulation. But our brains are set up to process the physical, as well as the audio and visual, signals associated with moving through the physical world. Since VR presents only audio and visual cues, the brain has to mimic its own physical cues. When the brain fails to do this, the user can develop the symptoms of motion sickness, as described earlier. When the brain succeeds in fooling itself, though, it sometimes cannot stop, even when the VR session is over. This phenomenon

Many head-mounted displays are designed to counteract the effects of cyberspace sickness that can strike VR users. Some HMDs, such as the Forte Technologies VFX1 Headgear shown here, flip out of the way, allowing users to take a "reality check." (Courtesy Forte Technologies, Inc.)

often leads to such problems as "virtual flashbacks," in which people suddenly feel that they are no longer in a physical environment. Such flashes frequently strike airplane pilots after simulator training sessions, which is why military pilots are not allowed into the air for at least a day after they finish such training.

Unfortunately, these types of physical problems are just par for the course of virtual reality. People have to decide whether their desire to work with virtual environments outweighs the discomfort that some virtual environment effectors cause. Future developments will probably eliminate many of these problems, and a few manufacturers are already incorporating some solutions into their products. Some head-mounted displays, such as the Forte Technologies VFX1 Headgear and the General Reality Cyber-Eye, have their screens on a hinge. VR users can thus lift the screens out of the way for a short "reality break" from their virtual environments.

Blurring the Definition of Reality

Another drawback that should be recognized is not so much a problem to be solved, as it is a question to be pondered: Is virtual reality a healthy thing to have? Many people are asking whether having computer simulations of the physical world, or simulated environments that are not possible in the physical world, will be good or harmful. If people spend enough time working and playing in virtual reality, they might not want to bother dealing with the real world. And the fact that the virtual environments they work and play in can be changed and reset at will could cause them to forget that actions in the physical world have long-lasting consequences.

The answers to these ethical questions will depend a great deal on how popular virtual reality becomes in the next few decades. But the history of another technology may give us a clue as to how virtual reality will end up. When the first modern televisions were produced in the 1930s, they were thought of much as VR is thought of today. Some people saw them as nothing more than expensive toys; others saw them as potential windows to the world that would lead to a golden age of information sharing and widespread education. And still others saw television as the tool that would destroy civilization as we knew it, wiping out the public's ability to think for itself.

These days, TV is primarily a form of entertainment, though people also use it as a news source and as a substitute classroom (via educational television and some cable networks). The only major debate regarding television centers on how it may be corrupting society through its depictions of sex and violence. Most of the discussions on how virtual reality might or might not be used seem to echo the early discussions about the role of television. Perhaps in 50 years, VR will occupy the same position TV holds today.

12
∇
A Virtually
Certain Future
for VR

*D*espite the drawbacks of virtual reality and hype-induced misunderstandings of its capabilities, VR promises to become an important part of future computing. People can already build basic VR systems for under $3,000, far less than the $250,000 Reality Built for Two system VPL Research sold in the late 1980s. More expensive systems, such as the CAVE or HMD-and-glove setups, have proven their worth in military, industrial, educational, scientific, and entertainment applications. A host of VR equipment manufacturers and virtual environment researchers have staked their money and their careers on expanding the ability of computers to mimic the physical world.

Of course, the drawbacks that do exist create doubts that VR will have much of a future at all. Some computer specialists and other experts see VR as nothing more than a toy that will have few, if any, lasting effects. Less skeptical experts believe that VR may have a useful place in computing, but that it will be decades before the technology improves to the point where people can use it full-time. But VR technology has made strong advances in its first decade, and there are indications that VR will have an equally strong future.

A Prediction of Virtual Prosperity

In the summer of 1996, Ovum Ltd., a British company that monitors trends in technology, predicted that virtual reality systems will have important roles to play in sales, financial management, and employee training by the beginning of the next millennium. Ovum also said that virtual reality companies will see their sales grow from the $135 million mark they set in 1995 to more than $1 billion in 2001.

Much of those future sales will come from desktop VR, combining the tools of virtual reality with personal computers such as those in millions of homes around the world. This is the type of inexpensive setup being used at Kelly Walsh High School in Casper, Wyoming, and in other schools around the United States. It bears the same relation to full-blown virtual reality systems, such as those being used in universities, that PCs have to the supercomputers that control high-end VR. Desktop VR systems will not offer the same type of fully immersive experience available with a CAVE system, and may not even meet the standard set by HMD-and-joystick virtual reality arcade games. But they will give their users the ability to do the types of intuitive, three-dimensional manipulations that separate VR from standard 2-D computing.

One unusual way of building virtual environments steps away from the idea of pulling VR users into the display. Quick-Time VR, a creation of Apple Computer Inc., uses a series of photographs to create a long panorama of a location in the real world. The photographs are made using a camera mounted on

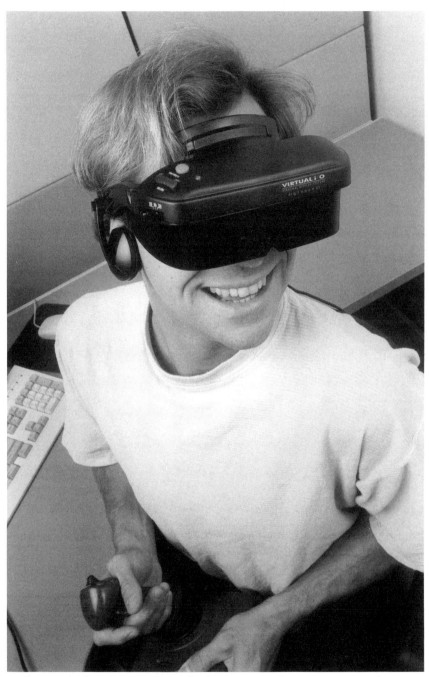

Desktop virtual reality systems, which promise to become a major factor in future VR development, are already available with current technology. (Courtesy Virtual i-O)

a pivot, to capture the scene as it might look to someone turning in a complete circle. The photos are then scanned into a computer and graphically stitched together. When the work is done, the entire circular view is spread across the computer screen like an unrolled label from a can of soup. The portion in the center of the screen represents the view in front of the user; the left and right sides of the display show equal portions of the rear view. Users can "turn around" or change to different viewpoints using a standard 2-D computer mouse.

Because QuickTime VR, as well as a similar product from Microsoft Corp. called Surround Video, are two-dimensional, they do not offer the sense of depth and immersion found in other displays. Thus, many people involved in virtual reality do not consider these panoramic environments to be "real" VR. On the other hand, these displays offer the ability to travel through and interact with the environments they replicate. Millions of computer users are satisfied with desktop PCs instead of multi-million-dollar supercomputers. Likewise, future VR customers may prefer the option of panoramic displays over fully immersive virtual environments.

A Virtual Presence in Simulated Spaces

Part of the future development of virtual reality will take place on the Internet, one of the many world-spanning networks of interconnected computers that have become the international shipping routes of the information age. Computer programmers are already working on ways to put three-dimensional environments on the World Wide Web, a subset of the Internet that makes heavy use of computer graphics. The most well-known method is a programming technique called Virtual Reality Modeling Language, or VRML (pronounced "*vermal*"). It is a three-dimensional counterpart to Hypertext Markup Language

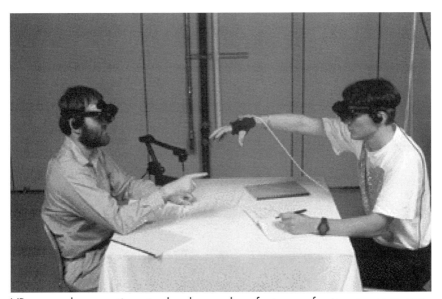

VR researchers continue to develop and perfect ways for two or more people to work in virtual environments at the same time. Here, researchers at the Human Interface Technology Laboratory work on the Shared Space project, which uses augmented reality to create interactive environments. (Courtesy Human Interface Technology Laboratory)

(HTML), which allows Web users to switch from one on-screen page of information to another using transfer commands contained in icons, on-screen buttons, and highlighted words or phrases. VRML sites use two-dimensional displays and a selection of simple mouse-and-keyboard commands to create the impression that users are moving through three-dimensional environments. The effect is similar to that of playing a video game without the need to score points or avoid monsters.

But VRML is even more of an infant technology than VR. As of the beginning of 1997, VRML sites were notorious for taking a long time to download from the Internet and for not working once they were loaded. And many people questioned whether VRML could really be considered virtual reality. It was not immersive: Its displays were presented inside computerized frames within the larger frame of a computer monitor. It did not allow for much, if any, interaction. VRML site visitors could

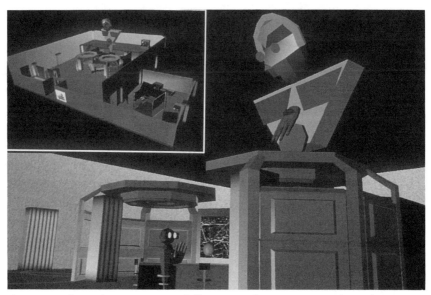

This image from the University of Illinois at Chicago's CAVE-based CALVIN (Collaborative Architecture Via Immersive Navigation) project is an example of how avatars can be used in virtual environments. The larger figure represents the avatar of a teacher who is guiding a student (the smaller avatar) through a virtual environment. (© 1996 Jason Leigh and Andrew Johnson, Electronic Visualization Laboratory, University of Illinois at Chicago)

decide whether they wanted to travel through objects or stop at their boundaries: Some sites contained links to other pages that looked like billboards or other objects on which visitors could click with their mouse pointers. But there were few, if any, options for handling objects or doing similar tasks. Computer industry experts agreed that while VRML might be of use in the future, it would need a lot of work.

In a sense, though, the landscape of virtual life on-line is already under development. People are already exchanging e-mail and selling products ranging from pizzas to T-shirts through the Internet. For years, Internet users have interactcd through Multi-User Dungeons (MUDs), originally created for fantasy role-playing games but quickly adapted as tools of communication. MUDs are text-only environments; the participants learn about each other only through the words they type. Thus, the participants can and do give themselves any name they wish and describe themselves any way they desire.

The graphics counterpart of the MUD is the MOO, the Multi-User Dungeon Object-Oriented. While MUDs are primarily designed for playing text games, MOOs are visual, virtual lands created with computer graphics. In such environments, participants construct buildings, gardens, mountains, and other counterparts to the physical world. Participants also interact with each other using *avatars*, computer-generated figures that take the place of the participant's body in the MOO. (The word "avatar" originally referred to the human or animal forms supposedly assumed by the gods of Hinduism during their brief visits on Earth. The term became associated with the graphical figures, as they are the temporary embodiment of their human controllers in the computer-generated environment.)

There are already a number of virtual worlds on the Internet in which people can share ideas through their avatars and construct their own minienvironments. These computer-generated "chat worlds" are perhaps the first step toward the type of widespread artificial architectural environments mentioned in Chapter Five. Such environments, promise their users the ability to navigate and interact with on-line information as easily as they walk through and do business in a shopping mall. These environments also have the added benefit of not restricting their users to mundane physical aspects such as gravity or weather. Depending on how an environment is programmed, participants can do just about anything they can imagine. The only real limits placed on participants, apart from guidelines on acceptable behavior, are the speed and power of their computers.

But MOOs also suffer from problems similar to those that afflict life in the physical world. Reports of various types of on-line crime have been coming from already-functioning MOOs. One such crime involves stealing heads of avatars from their users: A newcomer to an on-line world will meet an experienced and apparently friendly participant who lets the newcomer in on a little secret—the head of his or her avatar can be exchanged for a fancier custom model. The experienced avatar then offers to show the newcomer how to go through the head-change process. As the newcomer's avatar removes its head, the other participant steals the newcomer's head and vanishes from the world, leaving the newcomer headless in cyberspace.

Combining the Best of Both Worlds

Desktop reality simulators and artificial worlds are fine for some types of work and (more likely) play, but people will always have to work in the world. Virtual reality has proved its use as an engineering tool by cutting back the amount of real-world work that has to be done. Many companies have saved millions of dollars designing virtual prototypes for the machines they make. Even so, a lot of time and effort can be wasted in transforming computer-created prototypes into real products. Augmented reality, the technology that overlays three-dimensional graphics onto the physical world, promises to be as useful a tool for building these machines as VR is for designing them.

The aerospace industry is one of the leading institutions in the drive to perfect augmented reality as an everyday tool. A typical commercial airplane has thousands of miles' worth of wires, cables, fuel lines, and hydraulic lines that have to be precisely installed. In addition, the body and wings of an airplane are a complex system of girders, metal sheets, and connectors that all have to line up correctly. One of the trickiest tasks in assembling an airplane is correctly reading the blueprints that refer to the plane's millions of separate parts. And an equally tricky task in maintaining an airplane is correctly reading the manuals that refer to its intricately linked mechanical, electrical, and hydraulic systems.

Augmented reality assembly or maintenance rigs could help workers eliminate the need to switch their attention from their work to their blueprints and back again. A computer-

Steve Mann, a researcher with the MIT Media Lab's perceptual computing group, demonstrates a portable computer of the type that may one day be used for augmented reality displays.   (© 1995 Webb Chappell, Courtesy MIT Media Lab)

generated representation of a system's assembly instructions would be projected on a pair of work goggles over the system being assembled. By matching a few key points on the work surface with similar points in the instructions, the computer controlling the display would ensure that both the display and the physical objects lined up.

This is the goal of a number of programs being conducted by or with the assistance of major airplane manufacturers. One such program is being conducted by Dr. Ulrich Neumann, a computer scientist at the University of Southern California. His work focuses on using augmented reality to point out where workers need to drill holes in airplane parts. The system on which Neumann has been working can put a computer-generated image within .25-inch of where it needs to be—pretty good, considering the difficulty of programming computers to recognize physical objects. But the system takes up to 10 seconds to adjust itself to changes in position, which is too long a delay for useful work. Similar problems have cropped up in other programs, such as another airplane assembly project at Boeing Co., and a project aimed at speeding up vehicle maintenance for the military. This problem should disappear as computer technology improves and as researchers gain more experience in teaching computers how to overlap the physical and virtual worlds.

There are also less intricate tasks that can be eased by augmented reality. At the MIT Media Lab, some researchers have been adapting augmented reality to the mysteries of photocopier repair, using special display glasses to merge maintenance instructions with their view of the machine. Others have been developing a range of wearable computers that might aid people in their daily lives. Such a system could display a map directing visitors to museums or hotels; enhance the office of a clerical worker with virtual phone directories and message boards; or present architectural or structural data about various buildings to building inspectors or superintendents.

A Final Note

A rule of thumb in computer science, called Moore's law, once said that says computers double in power about every two years. That is, each new generation of computers worked twice as fast, could handle twice as many functions at one time, and in general was twice as good as those available two years before. (Gordon Moore, one of the cofounders of computer chip maker Intel Corp., first made this observation during the 1960s. In 1997, new developments in the industry made it likely that this "law" would be in effect for only a few more years.) Virtual reality, which is a combination of computers, hardware, and special software, seems to be following a slower but steadier path of development. But, as with all other technologies, virtual reality's path can always change, speeding up if researchers suddenly make a series of breakthroughs or slowing down if interest in a particular application wanes.

Virtual Reality: Computers Mimic the Physical World reflects the state of VR as it was at the beginning of 1997. The technology and the business of virtual reality have undoubtedly changed since then. HMDs may have improved, or computers may have developed to the point where lag times in rendering virtual environments are irrelevant. VR companies may have gone into or out of business. (For example, Virtual i-O, mentioned in this book, closed in the summer of 1997.) One of the best places to find out the most recent developments in VR is on the Internet, which itself seems to have a strong future. Searching the World Wide Web under the categories of "virtual reality" or "virtual environments" should yield enough information to satisfy anyone's curiosity. Otherwise, scanning newspaper and magazine listings, such as *The Reader's Guide to Periodic Literature* or computerized sources, should point the way to the most up-to-date information.

GLOSSARY

Terms in the glossary appear in *italics* the first time they are used in the text.

3DOF *See* three-degree-of-freedom.

6DOF *See* six-degree-of-freedom.

amplitude A measure of the amount of disturbance created by a wave. The amplitude of a wave on a lake, for example, is the distance between the top (crest) or bottom (trough) of the wave and the surface of the lake when it is calm.

application A computer program that enables a user to do a specific task. Word processors and games are types of applications.

artificial reality A computer display controlled by the interaction of the user's image with the displayed environment. This term was coined by computer scientist Myron Krueger.

augmented reality A computer display that seems to overlay computer-generated images onto physical world objects. Usually, this effect involves projecting the computer images onto a head-mounted display, a special pair of glasses, or a small monitor that hangs in front of one eye. The Sword of Damocles HMD was technically an augmented reality display.

autostereoscopic A computer display that can create the illusion of 3-D sight without requiring the user to wear special glasses or other equipment.

axis A mathematical term that refers to the three directions of movement in the physical world. The plural of axis is **axes** (pronounced "acks-eez"). The three axes are the X (left/right) axis; the Y (up/down) axis; and the Z (forward/back) axis. These three axes are also known as the Cartesian axes.

binocular parallax   The brain's ability to perceive three-dimensional depth and distance by combining the slightly offset images sensed by each eye.

bond   In finance, an agreement by a company or a government to repay loans made to that company or government. Usually, the term refers to the document that acknowledges the receipt of the loan and guarantees its repayment, with a specific interest payment, at the end of a fixed period.

cathode-ray tube (CRT)   A vacuum tube that forms images by shooting electrons from a negatively charged source (a cathode) to a phosphorescent screen that glows when hit by the electrons. Electromagnets inside the vacuum tube bend the beam, forcing it to rapidly scan across the surface of the screen. Color television sets and computer monitors have differently colored screens in the same CRT.

CD-ROM   *See* compact disc-read only memory.

circuit   A pathway for electricity formed by the wires in an electrical device.

circuit board   A board in a computer or other electronic device that houses microprocessors or other components connected by printed or etched wire circuits.

commodities   Goods, such as gold, wheat, oil, or livestock, that can be transported easily across country or overseas.

compact disc (CD)   A plastic-covered aluminum disc that contains digital information in the form of small pits etched into the disc's surface by a laser. CDs can be used to store either computer data or sound tracks. (CDs were created as a smaller alternative to 12- to 14-inch optical discs.)

compact disc-read only memory (CD-ROM)   A compact disc that contains text, audio, and visual computer files that can be read by a computer drive but cannot be altered.

computer graphics   Visual displays created using computers. A simple bar graph created with a word processor is technically an example of computer graphics. However, the term usually refers to more advanced displays, such as those in video games or flight simulators.

CRT   *See* cathode-ray tube.

cyberspace   The imagined world created by the Internet and other computer networks in which people communicate and share information. William Gibson, a science-fiction author, created the word in his 1984 novel *Neuromancer*.

database A collection of information stored as a computer file that is set up to allow people to easily retrieve that information.

desktop computer In general, any computer that can fit on top of a desk. *See also* personal computer.

effector Any device used to display or control a virtual environment.

electric potential The ease with which any material conducts electricity. Electric potential is measured in volts.

electromagnetic force In physics, the combined properties of electricity and magnetism. Electricity and magnetism are very similar forces: Every electric current generates a magnetic field, and every magnetic field can be made to generate an electric current. Because electricity and magnetism are so strongly linked, scientists consider them to be aspects of the same force. Other examples of electromagnetic force are light waves, radio waves, and microwave radiation.

fiber optics The use of optical fibers to transmit information.

flight simulator A device or computer program that reproduces the effects of airplane or helicopter flight.

force ball A stationary, ball-shaped effector that reacts to pushing and twisting forces applied to it by the user, letting the user navigate virtual environments.

force-feedback An effector that mimics weight, solidity, or other physical sensations through motorized resistance to a user's movements.

frequency A measurement of how many waves travel through a substance in a given amount of time. For example, humans can hear from as few as 15 to as many as 20,000 sound waves per second.

graphics board A microprocessor circuit board that is designed specifically to calculate and render computer graphics.

gyroscope A device that uses a rapidly spinning mass mounted in a freely moving framework to maintain its orientation.

gyroscopic tracker A position tracker that uses gyroscopes to detect which way a VR user moves.

haptic Related to the sense of touch.

head-mounted display (HMD) A computer or television monitor that rests on or otherwise attaches to the head of a user. HMDs can incorporate headphones and position trackers, and can provide either a semitransparent view (as in augmented reality) or a fully enclosed display (as with most VR systems).

▽

HMD   *See* head-mounted display.

hypertext   A computer programming technique that uses portions of a computer document as links to other documents. On a World Wide Web page, a hypertext link can be a short string of words, a simulated on-screen button, or a picture.

hypothesis   In science, a possible explanation for a physical phenomenon that needs to be proven by experimentation.

icon   A small picture used to represent a computer program. When selected, an icon activates the application it represents.

immersion   The sense of being totally surrounded by a virtual environment.

immersive   Capable of creating a sense of immersion in a virtual environment through programming techniques and/or a system of effectors.

integrated circuit   A complete electrical circuit—including wires, switches, and other components—that has been etched onto a single chip of material such as silicon.

interactive   Capable of conducting command-and-response interactions between users and computers with little or no time lag. Also, virtual environments capable of responding immediately to any changes the user makes.

interaural amplitude difference   The differing force with which sound waves hit each ear, depending on which ear is closer to the source of the sound waves.

interaural time difference   The short delay between the moment sound waves reach one ear and the moment they reach the other.

internet   A globe-spanning network of interconnected computer systems. Though it is the most well-known network, the Internet is actually just one of several networks that exist to help people exchange news and ideas with one another.

joystick   A post-shaped control device that allows movement in two of the three dimensions. A 3-D joystick allows movement in all three dimensions (forward/back, left/right, up/down).

lag time   The delay between an action and the effects of that action. In VR, lag time reflects how long it takes a virtual environment to catch up to a user's movement.

LCD   *See* liquid-crystal display.

LED   *See* light-emitting diode.

light-emitting diode (LED)   A diode is an electronic component that lets current flow in one direction but prevents it from flowing in the other. A light-emitting diode produces light as current flows through it. Unlike incandescent light bulbs, LEDs use very little energy.

liquid crystal   A normally transparent liquid material that turns opaque when an electric current runs through it.

liquid-crystal display (LCD)   A computer display made up of a liquid-crystal material trapped between separate layers of glass or plastic.

mechanical tracker   A position tracker that uses electronic linkages attached to mechanical joints to measure movement.

microcomputer   *See* personal computer.

microprocessor   A type of integrated circuit that contains a computer's master control circuitry.

monoscopic   A visual display that presents a single, two-dimensional image.

motion tracker   *See* position tracker.

mouse   A computer device that uses a rolling ball and at least one button to control an on-screen cursor. A standard computer mouse provides only two-dimensional (up/down, left/right) movement.

mouse, 3-D   A computer mouse used to navigate in three-dimensional computer environments.

nanometer   1 billionth of a meter, roughly 39 billionths (0.000000039) of an inch.

nebula   An immense cloud of dust and gas in space, usually caused by the explosion of a star.

optical fiber   A solid, very thin glass or plastic fiber that can transmit light around curves.

PC   *See* personal computer.

peripheral   In general, any device designed to put information into a computer (such as a keyboard or a mouse) or to get information out of a computer (such as a monitor or a set of speakers).

persistence of vision   A phenomenon of human sight. The eyes and brain retain an image of an object for a split second after that object leaves a person's line of sight. This image retention explains why people can watch a movie—really just a rapid series of separate images—and perceive a continuous flow of action.

personal computer   Any small computer generally used for home or office work, such as a laptop or desktop computer.

photoreceptor   A mechanical or electronic device, or a group of cells, that can detect light.

pixel From "picture element." A small block of color used to create a computer graphic image.

polarity The alignment of an electromagnetic force such as light waves. An example is the north-south orientation of a magnetic field.

polarization The separation of an electromagnetic force into different polarities.

polarizer Something that can separate polarities.

position tracker An effector that lets a VR system monitor which way a user moves his or her head, arms, legs, hands, or whole body. Position trackers can be **magnetic, sonic, mechanical,** or **gyroscopic**.

proprioception The ability of the body to sense its own movement and position through special sensory cells in the muscles, joints, and inner ear.

proprioceptor One of the special sensory cells the body uses to generate the cues of proprioception.

ray-tracing A way to determine how objects in a virtual world would be illuminated by calculating the path light rays would take from the viewer's eye to the objects. In effect, this method involves pretending to make light waves "back up" from the eyes to the objects in a virtual environment.

reality engine *See* reality simulator.

reality simulator A computer system specially designed to create and run VR simulations.

real time A computer's or a robot's ability to respond to its user's commands almost immediately.

refresh rate The number of times per second that a computer redraws the images it displays. VR systems need to maintain a refresh rate of 30 frames per second to create and maintain a sense of 3-D immersion.

render To create a computer graphic image, particularly a three-dimensional image.

semicircular canals Three fluid-filled tubes that form part of the inner ear and help the body maintain its balance. Each tube makes a half-loop along one of the **Cartesian axes**.

scanning probe microscope A microscope that can scan an extremely small object by passing a needle-like probe over its surface.

scientific method The process of explaining natural phenomena through observation, hypothesis, and experimentation. The scientific method also involves verification of one's work by other scientists.

securities Documents that indicate ownership (such as stocks) or acknowledge and guarantee repayment of a loan (such as bonds).

semiconductor A material that provides partial resistance to an electrical current flowing through itself.

semitransparent mirror A reflecting surface that lets the viewer see a reflected image overlaid on the view of objects behind the mirror.

shutter glasses A set of liquid-crystal lenses that rapidly flicker between transparency and obscurity in synch with a rapidly alternating left-eye/right-eye computer display. This method gives a good simulation of three-dimensional sight.

six-degree-of-freedom (6DOF) Allowing one to move along and spin around all three axes of the three-dimensional world.

sonic tracker A position tracker that monitors movement using tiny microphones that pick up ultrasonic pulses from a fixed emitter.

sound waves Disturbances in the air or other materials that humans can interpret as sound.

spatial sound Sound as it is heard in the physical world.

spreadsheet A computer accounting program that organizes financial data by placing it in categories in a series of columns and rows; also, a printed version of such a form.

stereoscope A device that uses two slightly offset pictures to create a three-dimensional image.

stereophonic sound Sound recorded with two or more microphones to give a more widespread effect.

stereoscopic vision The visual perception of length, width, and depth.

stock A share of ownership in a company; also, a document that represents such a share of ownership.

tactile feedback An effector that mimics physical sensations (such as how a brick wall feels) by stimulating the touch receptors in the skin. Inflatable air sacs or vibrating panels in a wired glove are some examples of tactile feedback.

teleoperation A technique of using virtual reality displays to operate remotely controlled robots or other machinery.

telepresence *See* teleoperation.

telerobotics *See* teleoperation.

texture map   A computer image, such as a photo of a textured surface, that can be pasted over a virtual object.

theory   A generally accepted explanation of a natural phenomenon.

three-degree-of-freedom (3DOF)   Allowing one to move along the three axes of the three-dimensional world but not to spin around them.

three-dimensional mouse (3-D mouse)   *See* mouse, 3-D.

transducer   Any device or material that converts one form of energy to another. For example, a radio speaker, which takes electrical impulses and converts them to sound waves, is a form of transducer.

transistor   An electronic component based around a semiconductor that can be used as a switch in an electric circuit.

ultrasonic   A sound wave with a higher frequency than that which humans can hear.

vacuum tube   A closed glass tube from which all air has been removed and which contains one or more electric wires. Vacuum tubes were used as switches in many early computers.

VCASS   *See* Visually Coupled Airborne Systems Simulator.

VET   *See* virtual environment technology.

VIEW   *See* Virtual Immersive Environment Workstation.

virtual   The word itself means something that exists in theory or in the imagination, but not in fact. Since the late 1970s, "virtual" has also come to mean just about anything that exists as a computer file or that can be accomplished using computer networks.

virtual architecture   This term has two general meanings. It can refer to a combination of computer hardware and software, including virtual reality, that is used to design buildings. It can also refer to a three-dimensional construct that mimics the function of a real-world building but exists only in a virtual environment.

virtual environment   A three-dimensional, immersive, interactive world designed for use in virtual reality.

virtual environment technology (VET)   Another term for **virtual reality**.

Virtual Immersive Environment Workstation (VIEW)   A project of the NASA Ames Research Center that was the first fully functional goggle-and-glove virtual reality system in the world. It was an expansion of the earlier **Virtual Visual Environment Display**.

virtual presence Another term for **virtual reality**.

virtual reality A form of computer technology that creates the effect of immersing its user in a three-dimensional, computer-generated artificial world.

Virtual Reality Modeling Language (VRML) A programming language that allows programmers to create three-dimensional environments that can be transmitted over the **World Wide Web**.

Virtual Visual Environment Display (VIVED) A project of the NASA Ames Research Center that created the first successful low-budget 3-D visual display.

visual tracker A position tracker that uses video cameras to monitor where and how users move in a physical space. Some institutions are working on visual tracker systems in which the users wear the cameras and the cameras gauge movement by tracing ceiling-mounted LEDs.

Visually Coupled Airborne Systems Simulator (VCASS) An experimental HMD system that displayed jet fighter controls and hostile territories as an easily comprehended virtual environment.

VIVED *See* Virtual Visual Environment Display.

VR *See* virtual reality.

VRML *See* Virtual Reality Modeling Language.

wand An effector that acts much like a 3-D mouse, but is shaped like a television remote control or a joystick without a base. Most wands house a **magnetic** or **gyroscopic position tracker.**

wave A pulse of energy that travels along or through something. There are two types of waves. *Transverse* waves, such as ocean waves, cause vibrations that are perpendicular to their path of movement. *Longitudinal* or *compression* waves, such as sound waves, cause vibrations that are parallel to their path of movement.

wired glove A glove-shaped effector that monitors the position of a user's hand and how far the user's fingers bend. Most wired gloves incorporate optical fibers to measure finger flex and have one or more position trackers, usually magnetic. Some wired gloves are rigged to provide tactile feedback.

World Wide Web (WWW) A subset of the Internet that presents information in a form that mimics pages from magazines.

workstation A very fast, very powerful personal computer designed specifically for advanced computer graphics or other projects that involve intensive calculations.

WWW *See* World Wide Web.

FURTHER READING

BOOKS

Billings, Charlene W. *Supercomputers: Shaping the Future*. New York: Facts On File, 1995. A companion to *Virtual Reality: Computers Mimic the Physical World* in the Facts On File Science Sourcebooks series, this book covers the development of computers from mechanical calculators of the 19th century to modern-day supercomputers. It includes a chapter on how supercomputers are used in virtual reality systems.

Eddings, Joshua. *How Virtual Reality Works*. Emeryville, Ca.: Ziff-Davis Press, 1994. A general overview of virtual reality that features abundant illustrations of how virtual reality systems work and of various ways in which VR is used.

Pimentel, Ken and Teixeira, Kevin. *Virtual Reality: Through the New Looking Glass*, 2nd edition. New York: McGraw-Hill, 1995. An adult-length but easily understood book that provides a highly detailed overview of the field of virtual reality, including lists of VR resources, manufacturers, and research institutions. Both authors are involved with the VR field, Pimentel at software firm Sense8 and Teixeira at computer hardware maker Intel.

Rheingold, Howard. *Virtual Reality*. New York: Simon & Schuster, 1991. An adult-length book considered a classic account of VR's history until 1991 and VR's early applications. Rheingold is widely respected for his writings on technology.

ARTICLES

Baum, David. "Assets in Wonderland," *Byte*, July 1995, pp. 111–117. A description of 3-D and VR financial market analysis software.

Chinnock, Chris. "Virtual Reality Goes to Work," *Byte*, March 1996, pp. 26–27. A straightforward, readable account of ways in which virtual reality may be used in business and on the Internet.

Gottschalk, Mark A., and Sharon Machlis. "Engineering Enters the Virtual World," *Design News*, November 7, 1994, pp. 52–63. A mid-1990s look at how VR could be used to help engineers design buildings, machines, and other projects.

Halfhill, Tom R. "See You Around," *Byte*, May 1995, pp. 85–90. A description of panoramic video technology, such as Apple Quick-Time VR and Microsoft's Surround Video applications.

Pountain, Dick. "VR Meets Reality," *Byte*, July 1996, pp. 93–98. A look at the tools being used to assemble and interact with virtual environments.

MAGAZINES

Unless otherwise noted, most of the magazines mentioned below can be found in bookstores, some record stores, and other retailers that have large periodical sections.

Computer Graphics World (CGW). Features articles on a wide range of graphics applications, including VR, film and television animation, CAD and other forms of modeling, and multimedia.

DV Magazine (formerly *Digital Video Magazine*). Similar to *CGW*, with a slightly greater focus on the use of computer graphics in animation and video games.

Graphic Exchange. More concerned with the nuts and bolts of creating computer graphics, and thus more suited for those with an interest in the technology itself. Its October/November 1996 issue featured different low-tech ways to create 3-D images, including old-fashioned red-blue filter glasses.

IEEE Computer Graphics and Applications. This is the journal of the IEEE Computer Society, a subgroup of the Institute of Electrical and Electronics Engineers. Though published mainly for university researchers and computer professionals, each issue contains many articles that non-professionals can easily understand. The best places to look for it are university libraries, especially engineering or computer science libraries, though it may also be found in larger public libraries.

3D Design. A readable though somewhat technical magazine that features articles on three-dimensional computer graphics techniques, including VR applications.

Wired. A monthly magazine that covers a broad spectrum of computer-related topics, including virtual reality and the Internet.

Virtual Reality Special Report. A bimonthly that featured articles on the entire VR industry. This magazine ceased publication in 1996 after a three-year run. However, used book and magazine stores may have back issues, as may some libraries.

INDEX

Italic page numbers indicate illustrations.

A

ALIVE (Artificial Life Interactive Video Environment) 50, 120, *120*
Ames Research Center (NASA) 29, 30, 32, 71, 75
Apple Computer Inc. 36, 146
arcade games 121–23
architectural modeling 53–59
Argonne National Laboratory 65, 74–75
Argonne Remote Manipulator (ARM) 65–66, *66*
Atari Research Center 31, 32
augmented reality 52, 86, 89, *149*, 152, *153*
avatars 104, *150*, 151–52

B

Bardeen, John 17
Bechtel Corp. 104
Bell, John T. 113–15
Bell Laboratories 17
Binocular Omni-Orientation Monitor (BOOM) 41, *76*, 77
binocular parallax 6, 15
Brattain, Walter 17
Bravo Multimedia 117
Brewster, David 11
Brooks, Frederick 26, 65
business meetings 103–6

C

Campbell, Dace 61, 62, 63, 139

Caterpillar 914G (wheel loader), and VR prototyping 78–79
cathode-ray tube display (CRT) 18, 30, 43, 142
CA-Unicenter TNG *105*
Cave Automatic Virtual Environment (CAVE) 50–52, *51*, *72*, 73, 74–75, *78*, 79, *111*, 119, 145, 146, *150*
Cinerama 13–14
Colt Virtual Reality 59–60
computer networks *105*
computer-aided design (CAD) 77
Convolvotron 32
Cosmic Worm 73
Crystal River Engineering 32
CyberEye HMD *42*, 143
cyberspace 5
cyberspace sickness 140–41

D

DataGlove 31–32, 36, 77, 110, 124
DataSuit 36
desktop virtual-reality systems 109–10, 123–24, *147*, 152
Dexterous Anthropomorphic Robotic Testbed (DART) 69–70, *70*
Dismounted Infantry Virtual Environment (DIVE) 130–31
Distributed Interactive Simulation (DIS) 128–29
Division Inc. *79*, 80
DOOM 120, 134–35
driving simulators 116–18, *117*
dVISE modeling system *62*, *79*

E

educational tool, VR as 109–15
Electronic Numerical Integrator and
    Calculator (ENIAC) 16
Electronic Visualization Lab (EVL)
    119
Emory University 95
employee training 115–16, 117,
    118–19, *119*, 146
Engineering Applications 58
Englebart, Douglas 18–19, 20
ergonomics 80–81, *81*
EyePhones 36

F

Fakespace, Inc. 41, 77
Falvo, Mike *66*, *67*
5th Glove *47*
financial industry 96–101, *98*, *100*, 146
Fisher, Scott 32
flight simulators 21–25, *22*, 44,
    115–16, 126–28, *126*, *127*
Fogler, H. Scott 113–15
force balls 48
force-feedback simulators 26–27,
    48–49, 65, *67*, 86
Forte Technologies VFX1 Headgear
    143, *143*
Furness, Thomas, III 24, 25, 29, 30, 126

G

General Electric Company *22*, 24
General Reality *42*, *47*, 143
Gibson, William 5
GLOWFLOW 27
graphics boards 8, *9*
"A Great Sandini Virtual Reality Cir-
    cus of the CAVE, The" 119–20
GROPE II 26–27, 65–66
gyroscopic trackers 40–41, 48

H

haptic devices 8, 48–49 *See also* force-
    feedback simulators
head-mounted displays (HMDs) 1–2,
    2, 8, 13, 14, 19–21, 24–25, 26, 27,
    29–35, 41–46, 69–70, 86, 92, 93,
    94, 95, 103, 110, 112, 119, 124,

127, 131, 138, 140, *143*, 145 *See
    also names of specific devices*
Heilig, Morton 13–14, 15
HMD Therapeutics 93
home gaming systems 123–24
house-shopping 106
Human Interface Technology (HIT)
    Lab 56–57, *56*, 61, *83*, *92*, 95, 112,
    126, *149*
Hunter, Ian 91

I

i-glasses 43, 90
ImmersaDesk 50
inertial trackers *See* gyroscopic trackers
Inman, Dean 93
interaural amplitude difference 45
interaural time difference 45
Internet 61, 150–51, 155
Iowa Driving Simulator (IDS) 116

J

J. Sainsbury 102
Joint Strike Fighter 128

K

Kaiser-Permanente Medical Group 94
Kawasaki Heavy Industries *117*, 118
Kelly Walsh High School 109–10, *110*,
    146
"Kids Room" *120*
Krueger, Myron 27–28, 29, 35, 50

L

Lanier, Jared 31–32, 35, 41
Learning Sites Inc. 113
LEEP Systems Inc. 30, 41
Lemson, Ralph 94
Li, Larry 69–70, *70*
Link Trainer 21, 23
liquid-crystal head-mounted displays
    30, 41, 43, 142

M

magnetic trackers 28–29, 32, 40, 48
manipulation devices 46–49 *See also
    specific devices*
Mars, exploration of 69–70

Massachusetts Institute of Technology
(MIT) 15, 18, 19, 91
Massie, Thomas 48–49, 66, 86
Mattel 110, 124
Maxus Systems International *98,* 99
McGreevy, Michael 29–31, 32
mechanical trackers 41
media hype 137–39
medical training 82–85
Metaphor Mixer *98,* 99, *99*
METAPLAY 27
meteorology 74–75
Microsoft Corp. 148
military training 125–35
MIST VR (Minimally Invasive Surgery
Training by Virtual Reality) 87–89
MIT Artificial Intelligence Laboratory
48, 66
MIT Media Lab 28, 32, 50, 120, *120,*
153, 154
Moondust 32
Moore's Law 155
motion trackers 28–29, 32, 39–41, *40,*
128 *See also specific devices*
motion-picture industry 4, 10–11
early attempts at immersion
11–12
and 3-D movies 12–14, 43, 44
and 3-D technology 12–13
Multi-User Dungeon Object-Oriented
(MOO) 151–52
Multi-User Dungeons (MUDs) 150–51

N

nanoManipulator system 66, *66,*
67–68, *67*
National Aeronautics and Space Administration (NASA) 29, 30, 41, 71, 75
Naval Postgraduate School 130, *130,*
131
Naval Research Laboratory 133, 134
navigational training 133
Neumann, Ulrich 154
Nintendo Entertainment System 110,
124

O

Omni-Directional Treadmill *130,*
131–32
Oregon Research Institute 93

P

Pantelidis, Veronica 111
Parkinson's disease 91–93, *92*
PHANToM manipulator 48–49, *49,*
66–67, *67,* 86
phobias 93–95
physical therapy 91–93
Polhemus Navigation Systems 28, 30
PowerGlove 109, 124
projection-based VR 27–28, 50–52,
51, 73, 84, 120, *120*
punch cards 17–18
"Put That There" (VR system) 28–29,
32

Q

Quantal International Inc. 99
Quicktime VR 146–48

R

Reagan, Ronald 61
real estate industry 106
Reality Built for Two (RB2, virtual-
reality system) 36, 145
reality simulators 8, 38, 39, 104, 152
retail industry 101–3
Riess, Tom 92–93, *92*

S

San Diego Convention Center 60
San Diego Data Processing Corpora-
tion 60
SANDBOX 73–74
Sandia National Laboratories 70–71
scientific method 71–73
Sensorama 14
Shockley, William 17
Silicon Graphics 36
Sitterson Hall (UNC building) 54–56,
55
Sketchpad 18, 19
SmartRoom 50, 120
sonic trackers 40, 48
sound-effect generators 7, 8
"Spider World" 95, *95*
stereoscope 10–11
STRICOM 130
SuperCockpit 25, 40, 126–28
surgical procedures 82

endoscopic surgury 87–88
  needle biopsies 89
Surround Video 148
Surveyor (lunar probe) 29
SURVIVE 120
Sutherland, Ivan 1–2, *2*, 15–16, 18,
  19–20, 24, 30, 40, 43, 52, 64
Sword of Damocles 19–20, *20*, 24, 27,
  30, 40, 43, 52, 64, 140

T
telepresence 68, 69, 70, 89
Telepresence Remotely Operated Vehicle (TROV) 71
three-dimensional glasses 43–44
  in motion pictures 12–13, 43
  mouse 47–48
  sound simulators 32, 45–46 *See*
  also specific devices
  and stereoscope 10–11, 13
tobacco mosaic virus 68
transistor technology 17
truck driVR 117
Turner Construction 57–58

U
"Ultimate Display, The" (Sutherland)
  19, 64
U.S. Air Force 127
U.S. Army Air Corps 21
U.S. Marine Corps 134–35
U.S. Navy 18, 21, 24, 133
Underwood, Becky 109–10
University of Illinois at Chicago 73
University of Michigan at Ann Arbor 113
University of North Carolina at Chapel
  Hill 26, 54–56, 65–68, 86
University of Pennsylvania 16
University of Southern California 154
University of Washington 56, 126
USS *Shadwell* 134

V
vacuum-tube technology 16–17
VEGAS (Virtual Egress Analysis and
  Simulation) 59
VICHER modules 114–15, *114*
VIDEOPLACE 28
View-Master 11

virtual architecture 61–63
Virtual Boy 124
Virtual Environments Laboratory,
  Northeastern University 118–19
Virtual Interactive Environment Work-
  station (VIEW) 32–35, *33, 34*, 36,
  37, 40, 41, 65, 75, 107
Virtual i-O 43, *90*, 124, 155
virtual offices 106–7
Virtual Presence 87
virtual prototyping 77–80, *78, 79*
Virtual Reality and Education Labora-
  tory (VREL), East Carolina Univer-
  sity 111–12
Virtual Reality Modeling Language
  (VRML) 148–50
Virtual Reality Roving Vehicle (VRRV)
  112
Virtual Reality Spacewalk/Orbiter 41
virtual teleconferencing 104–5
Virtual Vision 92, 124
Virtual Visual Environment Display
  (VIVED) 30–31, 32, 65
Virtual Windtunnel 75–77, *76*
Virtual World Entertainment 121–23,
  122
Virtuality *42, 117*, 118, 121
Visible Human database 84
visualization devices 41–45
Visually Coupled Airborne Systems
  Simulator (VCASS) 24–25, 29, 30,
  35, 40, 65, 126, 127, 128
voice-recognition devices 28, 32
VPL Research 32, 35–36, 41, 77, 110,
  124, 142

W
wands 48
Wayne State University 73
Weghorst, Suzanne 92
Wheatstone, Charles 10
Winchester Total Recoil 121
wired gloves 8, 31–32, 46, 47, *76*, 77,
  86, 145
World Wide Web 5, 61–62, 148–51, 155
Wright-Patterson Air Force Base 24

Z
Zimmerman, Thomas 31–32
Zyda, Mike *130*